The COUPON SAVER'S COOKBOOK

BOOKS BY BERYL MARTON

Out of the Garden, Into the Kitchen

Diet for One, Dinner for All

The Complete Book of Salads

The COUPON SAVER'S COOKBOOK

BERYL M. MARTON

CROWN PUBLISHERS, INC.   NEW YORK

Inquiries should be addressed to Crown Publishers, Inc.,

One Park Avenue, New York, New York 10016

Printed in the United States of America

Published simultaneously in Canada

by General Publishing Company Limited

Library of Congress Cataloging in Publication Data

Marton, Beryl.

The coupon saver's cookbook.

1. Cookery.   I. Title.

TX652.M294 1980   641.5′55   80-12168

ISBN: 0-517-541548 (cloth)

     0-517-54203X (paper)

Designed by Camilla Filancia

10 9 8 7 6 5 4 3 2 1

First Edition

CONTENTS ★★★★★★★★★★★★★★★★★★★★★★★★★

INTRODUCTION

Everyone loves a bargain, and the sensational growth of couponing in households all over America certainly proves it. Driven by inflation and the need to stretch our food dollars, we have formed countless refunding clubs, stuffed coupons by the dozens into odd shoeboxes, exchanged them with our neighbors, and enjoyed the friendly competition over who can save the most.

Less emphasis, perhaps, has been put on the problem of what we *do* with these coupons once we have them. Coupons for certain types of products seem to repeat themselves month after month, but a steady diet of cottage cheese and pineapple salads, gelatin molds, the same syrup over the same pancakes, or Toll House cookies made every week to use up your coupons for chocolate bits can get pretty boring. My Scottish background, and many years as a professional chef who had to maintain quality and keep costs low, led me to think along economical lines long before coupons had become a household word. As a cooking instructor, one of the first things I tell my students is, "Once you understand the basic principles of good cooking, don't be afraid to play around, try out, substitute, invent." Creativity is half the fun, providing it works! (For instance, veal piccata is a favorite with lots of people, but veal is quite expensive. Once, when I had a good buy on poultry, I worked out a chicken piccata that I don't pretend is the same thing, but it certainly disappeared off the table fast enough and now I often have to make it on request.)

In the best of all possible worlds, I would buy only the choicest veal, lobster and goose from the markets I know and trust, and the freshest vegetables and fruits—as would any good, professional cook who was on an unlimited budget. Compromise on the quality of ingredients almost always translates into some compromise in the quality of the final dish. But there are few Americans who are not feeling the effects of the shrinking food dollar. Making the most of couponing is, at least, one effective way to fight back.

Since couponing is now done by cooks at every level of knowledge from beginners to the most experienced, I have tried to include recipes to reflect a broad variety of tastes. Some dishes are quite simple to make, while others require more complicated techniques and are fairly sophisticated.

While the main objective of couponing is to save money, you will find that some recipes call for more expensive ingredients than others, and certainly not every dish in the book is a budget recipe. If you have saved a substantial amount on coupons for one or more staples, you may want to find a way of incorporating them into a new dish that requires buying a few additional ingredients. Just as the recipes were written for cooks with a wide variety of experience, so they will appeal to consumers with budgets that may vary from tight to generous.

HOW TO USE THIS BOOK

In compiling the book, I have organized the chapters by type of coupon offered, i.e., Coupons for Cereals; Coupons for Coffee, Tea, Cocoa, etc.; Coupons for Baking Ingredients. Within each of these chapters, the various types of recipes that can be made with these coupons are grouped together; as an example, within the chapter on Coupons for Fruits and Nuts, you will find Appetizers and Soups; One Condiment and Main-Course Dishes; Baked Goods and Desserts. (Naturally most recipes will contain more than one ingredient for which coupons are issued. The division into chapters is necessarily somewhat arbitrary, but I have generally categorized recipes by the ingredient that either adds to its special quality or presents an interesting variation on an old standard.) If you are simply looking for good main-dish ideas or good desserts, etc., go to the Index in the back where you can find all the recipes handily listed.

In every case, I have tried to make the instructions clear enough so that even a relatively inexperienced cook can turn out a foolproof Chocolate Bombe Mousse or a Puff Paste. *Notes* give helpful information about the recipe they follow; *Comments* are more general, with information on ingredients or techniques that may have applications in many recipes. I hope that this book will lead you to the kind of informed but relaxed kitchen creativity that often results in some of the most enjoyable meals.

NOTE ★★★★★★★★★★★★★★★★★★★★★★★★★★

The symbol ★ indicates the ingredient for which coupons are covered in that chapter.

A note on baking recipes: Microwave times are not given for cakes, pies or similar baked items. It is the author's belief that baked goods are far superior when baked in a conventional or convection oven.

COUPONS FOR DAIRY PRODUCTS

Manufacturers rarely issue coupons for *fresh* milk products; however, if you keep your eye on local supermarket ads, you will find occasional coupons issued toward the purchase of milk, butter and such specialties as yogurt and sour cream. Nonfat dry milk and canned milks, both condensed and evaporated, will comprise the bulk of your dairy coupons.

From a diet and health point of view, nonfat dry milk should be an important purchase on your staple list. It contains all the essential nutrients of whole milk, but eliminates butterfat, which is the cholesterol-forming ingredient objected to by many nutritionists. Those on restricted caloric intake will also benefit by its use both for drinking and in cooking. Large families with small children would be well advised to consider reconstituting the product according to package instructions and chilling it well before serving. If the nonfresh quality offends, mix it with half whole milk and stir well. Store in the refrigerator in covered 1-gallon containers. The savings will be considerable.

For those on restricted diets due to heart disease, diabetes or overweight, the American Heart Association recommends the use of nondairy cream substitutes readily available on the market today. The caloric intake is somewhat reduced. Light cream has 30 calories per tablespoon and imitation cream has 20. The animal fat ingredient is eliminated. These cream substitutes can be frozen and have a long refrigerator shelf life once opened. Commercial dessert toppings, as a substitute for heavy whipped and sweetened cream, are also recommended for specialized diets, as are safflower and corn-oil margarines. Butter and lard are high on the "not recommended" list for cholesterol-restricted diets.

Occasionally coupons are issued for products such as sour cream, yogurt, cheeses, margarines, dessert toppings, vegetable oils, etc. I have never seen coupons issued for fresh eggs; however, at certain times of the year eggs are cheaper. Baking to stock the freezer when cheaper eggs are available might be a good plan.

There are often coupons issued for egg substitutes; however, using them in baking is tricky. The properties of the egg are necessary in most baked products and must be replaced when using a substitute; therefore the advantage is lost. When you are eating the substitutes in the form of "scrambled" eggs or "omelets," you can enhance their quality with sautéed scallions or chopped or sliced mushrooms, or add chopped ham, salami or smoked salmon, just as you would to fresh eggs. You can also beat in cream or cottage cheese while scrambling, or use cheese to dot the top of an omelet before it sets. Grated Parmesan or Cheddar cheeses can also be used for this purpose.

Lard is rarely used in today's baking. It has had a bad press, probably because it contains so much cholesterol. However, it still makes the very best pastry. The most succulent berry and fruit pies I have ever eaten were made by a woman I knew when I was an adolescent. She managed a private hunt and gun club south of Montreal and was a marvelous, old-fashioned cook. She would never use anything but lard for her pastry. She made Cornish pasties that were absolutely mouth-watering, as was her Steak and Kidney Pie. She was in her late sixties when I knew her and her husband in his seventies; they were both going strong. No evidence of clogged arteries or high cholestrol count in those worthies, but then they did a lot of vigorous, physical work.

I am including a butter pastry to use as you deem fit. I am even including a puff paste made with sweet butter. Puff paste is a nuisance to make, but this recipe is a good one I evolved that really works wonders for special tarts and pastries.

In this chapter, there are recipes for appetizers and main-course dishes, soups and sauces and baked goods and desserts.

APPETIZERS AND MAIN-COURSE DISHES

MOZZARELLA WITH ANCHOVIES

This appetizer was dictated to me in the bar of my husband's ski lodge. The donor was one of the Italian delegates to the United Nations. We became fast friends. He and his wife supplied me with many family favorites, while I, in return, presented them with recipes I served in our restaurant.

★ 1 pound mozzarella cheese
2 cans (2 oz. each) oil-packed anchovies
1 loaf of Italian or French bread

Cut the mozzarella cheese into paper-thin slices. Heat the anchovies in the packing oil over low heat, beating with a whisk or fork until anchovies dissolve in the oil. Remove crust from the bread and cut it into ¾-inch-thick slices. Arrange a layer of bread in a shallow baking dish. Top with a layer of cheese. Repeat until dish is filled and all cheese is used. Pour anchovy sauce over top. Bake in a preheated 350° F. oven until cheese has melted. Cut into fingers and serve hot with cocktails. Yield: 12 servings.

CHEESE-MELBA TOAST

I made this toast with all the leftover homemade bread we accumulated during my restaurateur days. It was so popular we could not keep up with the demand.

1 small loaf of homemade
  bread
¼ pound (½ cup) butter or
  margarine, melted

1 teaspoon garlic powder
★ 1 cup grated Parmesan cheese

Slice bread paper-thin, then cut each slice into 4 pieces. Lay pieces on a cookie sheet. Brush with melted butter or margarine. Sprinkle with garlic powder, then with Parmesan cheese. Bake in a preheated 350° F. oven for 15 minutes, or until crispy and browned but not burned. Serve in baskets as an appetizer with drinks or as a bread course with dinner. Yield: approximately 64 slices.

SWISS CHEESE FONDUE

Traditionally, the Swiss ordain that a piece of bread dropped into the fondue pot by a lady guest permits the men in the room to steal a kiss.

★ 2 pounds imported Swiss
  cheese, shredded
2 tablespoons flour
2 cups dry white wine
1 garlic clove, crushed

salt and pepper
½ teaspoon grated nutmeg
¾ cup Kirschwasser
1 loaf of French bread, cut
  into 1-inch cubes

Mix cheese and flour. Heat the wine. Add cheese-flour mixture and garlic to the wine. Heat, stirring, until cheese melts. Add salt and pepper to taste, nutmeg and Kirsch. Turn into a ceramic fondue pot. Surround with bread cubes. Place on a low table, and provide fondue forks. Guests spear a bread cube, dip it into fondue, and pop into the mouth. Yield: 12 servings as an hors-d'oeuvre.

CURRY DIP

This recipe was sent to me by a Canadian friend from Toronto, and it is splendid looking and tastes delicious.

★ 8 ounces cream cheese
★ 1 cup grated Cheddar cheese
1 to 1½ ounces (2 to 3 tablespoons) sherry

1 tablespoon curry powder
1 cup Apple Chutney (p. 146)
2 tablespoons snipped chives, fresh or frozen

Soften cream cheese to room temperature, then beat well with Cheddar cheese. Beat in sherry and curry powder. Form into a mound and refrigerate for at least 8 hours. Just before serving, spread mound with chutney and sprinkle with chives. Serve with crackers. Yield: 12 servings.

PIZZA QUICHE

I racked my brains one day, trying to make a commercial frozen pizza go further and become more nutritious. The result is below.

1 frozen filled commercial pizza (13½ oz.) 9-inch size, defrosted
1 onion, chopped
1 ounce (2 tablespoons) butter or margarine
¼ pound mushrooms, sliced

3 eggs
1 teaspoon salt
freshly ground pepper
2 cups reconstituted nonfat dry milk
★ ¼ cup grated Cheddar or Parmesan cheese

Press the defrosted pizza into a pie plate (9 to 10 inches across). Sauté onion in butter until limp. Add mushrooms and sauté for 5 minutes. Cover pizza with these vegetables. Beat eggs with salt and pepper to taste. Beat in milk. Pour over onions and mushrooms. Sprinkle with cheese. Bake in a preheated 375° F. oven for 25 minutes, or until a knife inserted in middle comes out clean. Yield: 6 servings.

EMBELLISHED PIZZA

Adding to your pizza not only makes it go further, but makes it taste better to boot.

1 commercial frozen pizza (16 oz.)
4 frankfurters
1 can (2 oz.) anchovy fillets

1 cup commercial marinara sauce
★ ¼ pound mozzarella cheese, grated
oil

Place pizza on a cookie sheet. Cut frankfurters into 1-inch pieces and distribute evenly over surface. Cut anchovy fillets into small pieces and distribute evenly over surface. Pour sauce over all. Sprinkle with cheese. Brush crust with oil. Place in a 375° F. oven and bake until cheese melts and is bubbly. Yield: 4 servings.

CHEESE QUICHE AND VARIATIONS

Quiche can be made adequately with reconstituted nonfat dry milk. I defy anyone to know that the butterfat has been eliminated. If you are used to cream in your quiche batter, then you will notice the difference. Just bear in mind this quiche is far healthier for you.

★ ½ cup grated Cheddar or Parmesan cheese
1 prebaked 9-inch pie shell (see Note 1)
★ 2 cups reconstituted nonfat dry milk (see Note 2)

4 eggs, lightly beaten
1 teaspoon salt
freshly ground pepper
2 tablespoons chopped fresh parsley

Sprinkle all but 2 tablespoons cheese on the bottom of the prebaked pie shell. Beat milk into eggs. Add salt, pepper to taste and parsley. Pour into shell. Sprinkle with remaining cheese. Bake in a preheated 375° F. oven for 35 minutes, or until puffed and browned on top. Insert a knife in the middle of the quiche. If it comes out clean, remove quiche from oven. Let stand for 10 minutes before serving. Yield: 8 servings.

Note 1: To prebake a pie shell: Line a pie plate with pastry. Press a piece of aluminum foil down into the pastry. Fill foil with a pound of dried beans or peas. (This prevents shrinkage and warping of pie-crust.) Bake in a preheated 425° F. oven for 20 minutes. Remove from heat and carefully lift out foil and beans or peas. Pour dried vegetables into a jar and keep for future similar use. Cool before filling.

Note 2: Whole milk, half and half or light cream may be substituted for nonfat dry milk.

CLASSIC QUICHE LORRAINE

Sprinkle 6 strips of bacon, cooked and crumbled, or ¼ cup imitation bacon bits, in the bottom of the prebaked shell. Proceed with basic recipe. Or add 1 cup chopped ham in place of bacon.

CHICKEN, TURKEY OR VEAL QUICHE

Scatter 1 cup chopped cooked chicken, turkey or veal over bottom of shell. Proceed with basic recipe.

ONION, SHALLOT AND MUSHROOM QUICHE

Sauté 1 small onion and 2 shallots, chopped, in 2 tablespoons butter until limp. Add ¼ pound mushrooms (see Note), sliced, and sauté for 5 more minutes. Scrape into the bottom of prebaked shell. Proceed with basic recipe.

Note: I never use canned mushrooms. In my opinion they have no flavor and add a rubbery unattractive quality to the finished dish. Fresh mushrooms are so readily available today and are infinitely more desirable, why substitute?

GREEN VEGETABLE QUICHE

Scatter 1 cup chopped, cooked green vegetable (well-drained spinach, broccoli, asparagus, green beans) in bottom of shell. Proceed with basic recipe.

TOMATO QUICHE

Sauté 1 onion, chopped, in 1 tablespoon butter or margarine until limp. Peel 3 ripe tomatoes (see Note), then cut into ¼-inch slices. Drain on paper toweling. Place 1 layer of tomatoes in bottom of shell. Sprinkle with one third of the cheese in the basic recipe and one third of the onion. Repeat this process twice. Use 1½ cups milk for the custard. Pour custard mixture over tomatoes and proceed as above.

Note: To peel tomatoes: Bring a saucepan of water to the boil; drop tomatoes into water; count slowly to ten. Remove tomatoes from water and peel. Skin will easily slip off. Peel peaches this way also.

CHEESE SOUFFLÉ MADE WITH NONFAT DRY MILK AND VARIATIONS

Soufflés made with reconstituted nonfat dry milk are wonderful for diets. You cannot tell that the butterfat has been eliminated from the milk product. When you are on a diet, reduce butter in the recipe by half, then proceed as instructed.

4 ounces (8 tablespoons) butter or margarine
★ 13 tablespoons grated Parmesan cheese
3 tablespoons flour

★ 1 cup reconstituted nonfat dry milk or whole milk, scalded
4 egg yolks
salt
freshly ground pepper
5 egg whites

Soften 2 ounces (4 tablespoons) of the butter or margarine. Use some of it to coat heavily a 1½-quart soufflé dish. Tie an aluminum foil cuff around top of soufflé dish to the height of 2 inches (see Note). Coat the inside of the foil cuff with the rest of the softened butter or margarine. Sprinkle the inside of the dish and cuff with 3 tablespoons of the Parmesan cheese. Set aside.

Melt 1½ ounces (3 tablespoons) of butter or margarine in a heavy-bottomed 1½-quart saucepan. Add flour and cook, stirring, for 2 to 3 minutes. Off the heat, beat in the scalded milk with a wire whisk. Return to heat and cook, stirring, until sauce is very thick. Remove from heat and add egg yolks, one at a time, beating vigorously after each addition. Stir in 1 teaspoon salt, pepper to taste and 8 tablespoons grated cheese. Dot with remaining 1 tablespoon butter or margarine. Swirl butter around to cover the surface of the soufflé base completely with fat. Cool to tepid. Soufflé can be prepared ahead, to this point.

Just before baking, beat egg whites with a dash of salt until stiff but not dry. Stir 1 large spoonful of the whites into the soufflé base. Fold remaining whites in very carefully. Turn batter into prepared soufflé dish. Sprinkle with the last 2 tablespoons of cheese. Bake in a preheated 375° F. oven for 45 minutes. Serve at once. Yield: 4 to 6 servings.

Note: Soufflés have a tendency to rise quite high. If no cuff is attached, soufflé batter can spill over the top and burn on the bottom of the oven.

Comment: Soufflés should be well puffed and brown on top. To serve, remove cuff; stick 2 forks into the center; tear soufflé into portions. Serve immediately before the puff settles. If slightly runny in the center, do not despair, many aficionadas consider this desirable; the runny part substitutes for a sauce.

Microwave Cooking: Use a glass or ceramic casserole. Sprinkle with paprika to add color to final dish. Bake on "medium" setting for 4 minutes. Turn dish and bake another 4 minutes, or until puffed and hot.

SEAFOOD SOUFFLÉ

Add 1 cup chopped cooked lobster, crab, scallops, shrimps or clams to the soufflé base before adding egg whites.

GREEN VEGETABLE SOUFFLÉ

Add 1 cup chopped cooked asparagus, well-drained spinach or broccoli to soufflé base before folding in egg whites.

CHICKEN OR TURKEY SOUFFLÉ

Add 1 cup chopped cooked chicken or turkey to soufflé base before folding in egg whites.

MUSHROOM SOUFFLÉ

Saute ½ pound mushrooms, chopped, in 1 ounce (2 tablespoons) butter. Add to soufflé base before folding in egg whites.

POTATO-CHEESE PIE

This Swiss dish was given to me by a young woman in return for one of my recipes. She insisted you *must* have imported Swiss cheese, but I have made it with domestic Swiss and even Vermont Cheddar when in a pinch; it always tastes fabulous. This pie is rich, so plan for small portions.

4 or 5 Idaho potatoes
★ 1 pound Swiss cheese
salt and freshly ground pepper

1 cup heavy cream
2 tablespoons chopped fresh parsley

Grease a 2½-quart casserole. Peel potatoes and boil until barely tender. Cut potatoes into ¼-inch slices. Place a layer of potatoes in the bottom of the casserole. Cover with a very thin layer of Swiss cheese. Sprinkle with salt and pepper to taste. Repeat until casserole is filled. Pour cream over top. Bake in a preheated 350° F. oven for 30 minutes. Sprinkle with parsley and serve. Yield: 8 servings.

SILKY SALMON CUSTARD

Canned salmon is no longer an inexpensive way to serve a family; however, it is still cheaper than fresh fish.

2 eggs, slightly beaten
★ 1 cup evaporated milk
salt and pepper
½ teaspoon paprika
1 pound canned salmon,
  flaked, bones removed

2 packages (10 oz. each)
  frozen peas, cooked
  according to package
  instructions
1 ounce (2 tablespoons) butter
½ teaspoon crumbled dried or
  1½ teaspoons minced fresh
  basil

Beat eggs, milk and seasonings to taste together. Fold into flaked salmon. Heavily grease a 1½-quart ring mold. Turn salmon into mold. Set mold in a shallow dish of hot water. Bake in a preheated 350° F. oven for 30 to 35 minutes, or until a knife inserted in middle comes out clean. Meanwhile prepare peas. Toss with butter. When salmon mold is cooked, place a heated plate over top of mold. Holding plate and mold together, quickly invert to unmold. Fill cavity of mold with hot buttered peas. Sprinkle with basil. Serve at once. Yield: 4 servings.

SOUTHERN FRIED CHICKEN WITH WHITE SAUCE

"White gravy" or sauce is a traditional accompaniment to fried chicken in many parts of the South. I add chicken flavoring to give zip to the sauce.

1 frying chicken, 3½ pounds,
   cut into serving portions
★ 2 cups reconstituted nonfat
   dry milk
1 teaspoon salt
freshly ground pepper
1½ cups all-purpose flour
2 eggs

4 tablespoons water
vegetable oil
2 ounces (4 tablespoons)
   butter or margarine
2 teaspoons instant chicken
   base powder or 2 bouillon
   cubes
2 tablespoons chopped fresh
   parsley

Wash chicken thoroughly and pat dry on paper toweling. Place in a deep bowl. Pour milk over chicken and let stand for at least 2 hours. Remove chicken from milk and again pat dry. Reserve milk for white sauce. Mix salt, pepper to taste and flour, reserving 4 tablespoons for sauce. Beat the eggs with the water to make an "egg wash." Dip chicken into egg wash, then roll in the flour mixture. Pour oil 2 inches deep into a deep chicken fryer or skillet. Heat to sizzling hot, 375° to 400° F. on a frying thermometer. Place floured chicken in hot fat and cook until brown and very crispy on all sides. Drain on paper toweling in a 200° F. oven while making sauce. Yield: 4 servings.

White Sauce

Melt butter or margarine in a small, heavy-bottomed saucepan. Scald the milk used to soak chicken. Use the 4 tablespoons of seasoned flour reserved from coating chicken. Sprinkle flour over melted butter or margarine and cook, stirring, for 2 to 3 minutes. Off the heat, pour in scalded milk all at once, beating vigorously with a wire whisk. Return to heat. Add chicken base powder or bouillon cubes and parsley. Cook, stirring, for 5 minutes. Pour over chicken at time of service. Yield: 2 cups sauce.

SOUPS AND SAUCES

SOUPS ★★★★★★★★★★★★★★★★★★★★★★★★★★★★

CHEDDAR-CHEESE SOUP

I make this soup with Vermont Cheddar. Having lived in Vermont for 9 years, I am somewhat prejudiced. I believe the Vermont cheese is the very best Cheddar you can obtain anywhere.

1 ounce (2 tablespoons) butter
  or margarine
2 tablespoons flour
★ 1 quart reconstituted nonfat
  dry milk, scalded
1 garlic clove, crushed
⅓ cup dry white wine

★ 1½ cups grated Cheddar
  cheese
1 teaspoon salt
freshly ground pepper
dash of grated nutmeg
1 egg yolk
2 tablespoons heavy cream
snipped chives, fresh or frozen

Heat butter in a good-size heavy-bottomed pot. Add flour and cook, stirring for 2 to 3 minutes. Off the heat, beat in milk and garlic. Cook, stirring, for 5 minutes. Add wine, cheese and seasonings to taste. Cook, stirring, until cheese melts and soup is smooth. Beat egg yolk with cream. Beat a small amount of hot soup into egg and cream mixture. When egg is thoroughly warmed, stir into soup. Heat, do not boil (see Note). Serve with a sprinkling of chives on top. Yield: 8 to 10 servings.

Note: Sauces with the addition of egg yolk as an enriching agent should be heated to just under the boiling point to eliminate any chance of the egg yolks scrambling and causing the sauce to curdle.

BACON AND CHEESE GARNISH FOR SOUPS

This recipe is based on a French garnish from Provence called a *pistou*. Traditionally it is made with garlic, basil and olive oil. My adaption is personal, and the bacon, garlic and cheese combination makes it somewhat heartier. Place a small bowl of the garnish in the center of the table and allow people to beat a teaspoon at a time into their individual servings.

2 strips of bacon, cooked
2 raw egg yolks
3 tablespoons olive oil
3 garlic cloves

★ ½ cup grated Parmesan cheese
1 to 2 tablespoons hot soup

One really needs a food processor or blender for this garnish. Place all ingredients except hot soup in the container of the machine. Blend until well mixed. Add hot soup to make a thick paste. Scrape into a small bowl and serve with soup. Yield: ¾ cup.

PESTO

This is an Italian garnish, especially popular around Genoa. Many Mediterranean dishes call for the addition of garlic and olive oil to the ingredients. *Pesto* is no exception. When fresh basil is in season, make loads of *pesto* and freeze it for future use. It is delicious with heavy vegetable soups such as minestrone. Serve in the same way as the Bacon and Cheese Garnish. This is a pungent and flavorful addition to soups and also makes an excellent pasta sauce.

1 quart fresh basil leaves, chopped
½ cup olive oil
1 cup pignolia or pine nuts

3 garlic cloves, crushed
salt and pepper
★ grated Parmesan cheese

Place basil, oil, nuts, garlic, salt and pepper to taste in the bowl of a food processor or blender. Blend until well mixed. Add cheese until you have a thick paste. Yield: 2 cups.

Comment: In making either Bacon and Cheese Garnish or *Pesto,* if you have neither a blender nor food processor, mince all ingredients by hand and beat in oil and cheese until you have a paste. In the case of Bacon and Cheese Garnish add soup at the last minute.

SAUCES

BÉCHAMEL SAUCE

★ 2 cups reconstituted nonfat dry milk, or whole milk

2 ounces (4 tablespoons) butter or margarine

4 tablespoons flour

1 teaspoon salt

¼ teaspoon white pepper

Scald the milk. Heat butter or margarine in a small heavy-bottomed saucepan. Add flour and cook, stirring, for 2 to 3 minutes. Remove from heat. Pour milk onto *roux* (see Note) all at once, beating vigorously with a wire whisk. Add salt and pepper. Return to heat and cook, stirring, for 3 to 4 minutes. Yield: 2¼ cups.

Note: A *roux* is a combination of fat and flour cooked together, before a liquid is added, until the flour absorbs all the fat.

MORNAY SAUCE

1 recipe Béchamel Sauce (preceding recipe)

★ ¾ cup grated Cheddar or Parmesan cheese (see Note)

dash of grated nutmeg

Stir cheese into sauce and heat until melted. Add nutmeg. Yield: 3 cups.

Note: I prefer Cheddar to Parmesan. It is less salty. Add no salt if using Parmesan until after the cheese has been stirred in. Taste before seasoning. If sauce is too thick with addition of cheese, dilute with more milk.

HOLLANDAISE SAUCE

Few people make hollandaise sauce by hand today. To do so you must first clarify the butter. This is done by heating the butter until the casein and the whey separate from the butterfat and the clear oily butterfat can be poured off for use in cooking.

4 egg yolks
juice of 1 lemon
dash cayenne pepper

pinch salt
★ ½ cup clarified butter, boiling

Place egg yolks in the bottom of a large bowl. With a wire whisk, beat vigorously over hot water until egg yolks are thick and lemon colored. Beat in lemon juice, pepper and salt. Beating constantly over hot water, beat in the boiling butter, gradually, until the sauce is thick and smooth. Serve at once. Yield: approximately 1 cup.

QUICK HOLLANDAISE SAUCE

To make this hollandaise one needs a blender or food processor.

4 egg yolks
dash cayenne pepper
juice 1 lemon

★ 4 ounces (8 tablespoons)
butter, boiling
salt

Place egg yolks, cayenne and lemon juice in the container of a blender or the bowl of a food processor. Blend. With machine running, very slowly pour in as much of the boiling butter as needed to thicken the egg yolks. Keep warm over hot, not boiling, water. Sauce will thicken considerably as it stands. Yield: 1 cup.

BAKING AND DESSERTS

Margarine is not really a dairy product, but it is always sold in that section of the market so I am including it here. There are many coupons issued for margarine; fewer for butter and lard. If you wish to use lard, just substitute for the shortening. The two recipes that follow are for butter-flavored pastries.

PÂTE BRISÉE

2 cups all-purpose flour
★ 6 ounces (¾ cup) cold sweet
    butter
¼ teaspoon salt

1 teaspoon sugar
1 egg yolk
4 tablespoons ice water

Place flour in a bowl. Cut in the butter until the mixture is crumbly. Add salt and sugar. Stir in egg yolk and enough water to make a stiff dough. Form into a ball. Refrigerate until ready to use. Yield: pastry for two 1-crust pies or one 2-crust pie.

Comment: The French make a well in the center of the flour, drop the butter, seasonings and egg yolk into the well and work it together with the fingertips before adding the water. I find our American way easier. Using a food processor, of course, is the absolute easiest: Merely place all ingredients except liquid in the processor bowl. Process and add liquid *only* until dough leaves sides of bowl.

PUFF PASTE

This recipe can be made with margarine rather than butter, but it is infinitely better with butter. The consistency and flavor of butter seem to make the difference.

1½ cups all-purpose flour
1⅓ cups cake flour
★ 1½ ounces (3 tablespoons)
   plus 12 ounces (¾ lb.) sweet
   butter

½ teaspoon salt
½ cup ice water

Sift all-purpose flour and cake flour together twice. Remove ½ cup and set aside. Cut 1½ ounces (3 tablespoons) butter into remaining flour. Add salt and enough water to make a sticky dough. Turn out onto a floured board and knead for 15 to 20 minutes. Roll into a pillow shape and wrap in waxed paper. Refrigerate for 40 minutes.

Meanwhile, knead the 12 ounces (¾ pound) sweet butter lightly. As bubbles of water exude, blot up with a paper towel. When much of butter's water has been kneaded out, knead in the reserved ½ cup flour. Pat onto a rectangle 5 x 3 x 1½ inches. Wrap in waxed paper and refrigerate. When dough and butter both feel of equal consistency, they are ready to work.

Cut a cross in the ball of dough. Roll out to a clover shape as shown in Diagram 1. The center pad should be thicker than the 4 leaves. Place butter on the pad in the center. Fold leaves over butter, pinching edges to secure. If butter has softened, sprinkle the package with flour, wrap in waxed paper and refrigerate. Otherwise, roll out to a rectangle 16 x 8 inches. (see Diagram 2.) *Do not let butter break through dough.* Fold the rectangle into thirds; turn so that the long edges go away from you and the triple fold faces you. (This is called a "turn.") Roll out again to a rectangle 16 x 8 inches. Refold, wrap in waxed paper and refrigerate for 40 minutes. Repeat this whole "turning" and refrigerating process 4 times. Let pastry rest for 2 hours before using as desired.

DIAGRAM 1

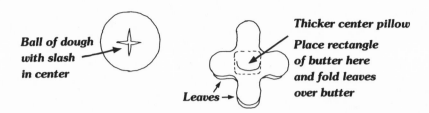

Ball of dough
with slash
in center

Thicker center pillow

Place rectangle
of butter here
and fold leaves
over butter

Leaves →

DIAGRAM 2

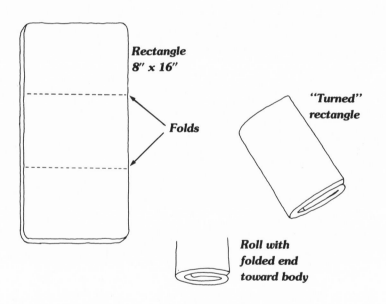

Rectangle
8" x 16"

Folds

"Turned"
rectangle

Roll with
folded end
toward body

Comment: Puff paste can be frozen and defrosted. Tarts made with puff paste are superior to those made with regular pastry. If you wish to make your own tart shells for such recipes as Seafood in Pastry Shells (see Index), follow instructions that follow. The "elephant ears" are wonderfully good.

PUFF PASTE TART SHELLS

Roll out the completed and rested pastry. Cut a circle with a large glass or a cookie cutter. Cut 2 more circles with a doughnut cutter of the same diameter. Wet the first circle around the edges. Lay a doughnut-shaped circle on top. Wet the edges of the first doughnut-shaped circle and place the second one on top of the first. Bake in a preheated 375° F. oven for 5 minutes. Reduce heat to 350° F. and bake for 30 minutes longer.

DIAGRAM 3

← **2nd ring**
← **1st ring**
← **Bottom circle**

Comment: Pastry will puff to almost double in size, and butter will ooze from pastry during baking period. Keep heat low rather than high to prevent scorching of the butter. The inner circles from the doughnut cutting can be baked together to make a cap for the pastry shell if so desired.

ELEPHANT EARS

Roll pastry into a rectangle 8 x 6 inches and ¼ inch thick. Sprinkle liberally with granulated sugar. With a wide edge facing you, roll the 6-inch edges toward the center like an open book. Fold together, then cut ¼-inch slices. Place 2 inches apart on a cookie sheet. Bake in a preheated 350° F. oven for 25 to 30 minutes. Yield: 32 small elephant ears.

Note: If you want large elephant ears, make the rectangle 16 x 8 inches and ½ inch thick.

DIAGRAM 4

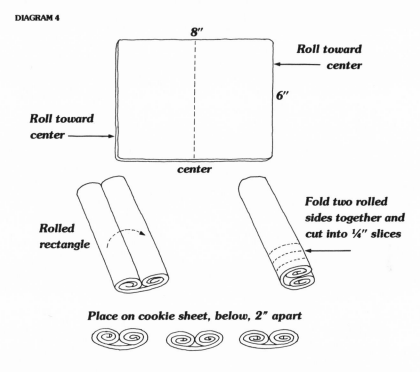

Place on cookie sheet, below, 2" apart

MELOPITTA

This is a great Greek dessert. All Mediterranean countries seem to have a honey-cheese pie. This one seems similar to the French *tarte au miel.*

pastry for 1-crust 9-inch pie	2 eggs
2 tablespoons dry bread crumbs	½ cup honey
	¾ cup raisins
★ 6 ounces cream cheese	grated nutmeg
★ 1 cup cottage cheese	1 tablespoon sugar

Fit the pastry into a 9-inch pie dish, and sprinkle the bread crumbs on the bottom of the pastry. Beat cream cheese, cottage cheese, eggs, honey and raisins together. Pour into the pastry-lined dish. Sprinkle with nutmeg and sugar. Bake in a preheated 425° F. oven for 15 minutes. Reduce heat to 350° F. and bake for a further 25 to 30 minutes. Cool completely before serving. Yield: 8 servings.

CINNAMON SWIRL BREAD

This is an excellent tea bread or coffee cake. Toasted, it is reminiscent of cinnamon toast.

1 cup boiling water
2 tablespoons sugar
2½ teaspoons salt
1 tablespoon margarine
★ 1 cup evaporated milk

2 packages active dry yeast
¼ cup tepid water (105° to 115° F.)
6 cups flour
6 tablespoons brown sugar
1 teaspoon ground cinnamon

Pour boiling water over sugar, salt and margarine. Add evaporated milk and cool to lukewarm. Sprinkle yeast over tepid water. When yeast is dissolved, add to the first mixture. Beat in enough flour to make a stiff dough. Turn out on a floured board and knead until smooth and elastic, 6 to 8 minutes. Form into a ball and place in a large greased bowl. Turn once to grease top. Cover with plastic wrap and allow to rise (see Comment) until doubled in bulk.

Punch down. Turn out onto a floured board and knead again for 1 to 2 minutes. Divide dough into 2 portions. Roll each portion into a 9-inch square. Sprinkle with brown sugar and cinnamon. Roll up as you would a jellyroll. Place in 2 greased loaf pans, 8 x 4½ x 2½ inch. Allow to rise until doubled in bulk. Bake in a preheated 425° F. oven for 15 minutes. Reduce heat to 350° F. and bake for 25 minutes longer. Yield: 2 loaves.

Comment: Bread dough should be set to rise in a very warm, draft-free spot. The top of a refrigerator or on top of an old-fashioned radiator is excellent. Another good place is inside an unlit gas oven with a pilot light. Place the bread on the second shelf and put a pan of boiling hot water under it. Close the door and allow dough to rise. You can tell when the dough has risen to full capacity by sticking a finger into the dough. If the impression remains without filling in, the dough is ready.

BLUEBERRY TAPIOCA

★ 2 cups reconstituted nonfat
   dry milk
⅓ cup sugar
½ cup quick-cooking tapioca

3 eggs, separated
1 teaspoon vanilla extract
2 cups fresh blueberries

Mix milk, sugar and tapioca in a small saucepan. Cook over medium heat, stirring, until tapioca is clear. Beat egg yolks in a small bowl. Beat a small amount of the hot tapioca mixture into egg yolks. Stir the warmed eggs into tapioca mixture. Cook over low heat, stirring constantly, for 5 minutes. Stir in vanilla. Cool. Beat egg whites until stiff. Fold into tapioca. Fold in blueberries. Serve. Yield: 6 servings.

BREAD PUDDING

My sister makes this fine custardy bread pudding. It is very English.

★ 3 cups reconstituted nonfat
   dry milk, scalded
3 egg yolks, lightly beaten
2 cups soft bread cubes
1½ cups diced peeled apples
½ cup raisins

½ cup sugar
dash of grated nutmeg
¼ teaspoon ground cinnamon
3 egg whites, at room
   temperature
⅓ cup sugar
¼ teaspoon cream of tartar

Stir scalded milk very slowly into egg yolks. Add bread cubes, diced apples, raisins, ½ cup sugar, nutmeg and cinnamon. Mix well. Pour into a greased 2-quart casserole. Bake in a preheated 325° F. oven for 50 minutes.

Beat egg whites until soft peaks form. Gradually beat in ⅓ cup sugar and the cream of tartar. Beat until meringue is very stiff. Spread over pudding, sealing the meringue to the edge of the casserole. Return to oven and bake until meringue browns lightly. Yield: 6 servings.

COUPONS FOR CEREALS

There seem to be more coupons issued for cereals than for almost anything else, other than baking products. This includes natural and sweetened dry cereals as well as grains to be cooked as hot cereals.

I find hot instant cereals hard to incorporate in recipes. The sweetening and spice additives make their uses questionable. My only suggestion is to add things to them, rather than the other way around. How about adding dried fruits and nuts, or chopped fresh fruits such as apples and pears? The unsweetened cooked cereals can be used many ways, as can dry cereals, both natural and sweetened.

This chapter gives recipes for main-course dishes, breads and pancakes and desserts. The dry cereals can always be substituted for each other. Just remember to substitute sweet for sweet and natural for natural, i.e., cornflakes for Grape-Nuts Flakes, Rice Chex for Wheat Chex, Frosted Flakes for Froot Loops, etc. Cooked cereals cannot be substituted. There is a vast difference between rolled oats and cream of wheat, for instance; if a recipe calls for a specific cereal, that texture and quality is the requirement. Substituting another cereal would spoil the final result.

Your aim is to use the issued coupons that are current. Read the following recipes and adapt your coupon purchases whenever possible. Use a little ingenuity and enjoy yourself.

MAIN-COURSE DISHES

COMPANY CHICKEN BREASTS

Chicken breast dishes are the best thing for entertaining. If you can learn to bone your own, or buy whole chickens when they are on sale and separate and store the breasts, you can entertain very elegantly for very little money. More can be done with chicken than any other meat. The breasts, or *suprêmes* as the French call them, are most versatile. This recipe is just one example of their use.

2 cups commercial sour cream
juice of 1 lemon
4 teaspoons Worcestershire
   sauce
1 teaspoon celery salt
2 teaspoons paprika
1 garlic clove, crushed
1 teaspoon salt

freshly ground pepper
3 pounds whole chicken
   breasts, halved and boned
★ 1½ cups cereal flakes, crushed
   (cornflakes, Grape-Nuts
   Flakes, Rice Chex, etc.)
4 ounces (½ cup) melted
   butter

Combine first 7 ingredients with pepper to taste. Add chicken and stir to coat pieces evenly. Refrigerate, covered, for at least 8 hours. Roll each breast in the cereal crumbs. Place in a shallow casserole. Drizzle with melted butter. Bake in a preheated 350° F. oven for 30 minutes. Yield: 6 servings.

BAKED CHICKEN

This is a quick, easy way to prepare chicken, and always popular. The garlicky, cheesy quality is appealing. It is fairly rich, so don't serve it to those who are dieting.

★ 2 cups crushed cornflakes, or dry cereal of your choice
½ cup grated Parmesan cheese
¾ teaspoon garlic powder
1 teaspoon salt

freshly ground pepper
½ cup chopped fresh parsley
1 frying chicken, 3 pounds, cut into serving pieces
8 ounces (1 cup) melted margarine

Mix cornflakes, cheese, garlic powder, salt, pepper to taste and parsley. Dip chicken into melted margarine, then roll in crumb mixture. Lay pieces side by side in a shallow baking dish. Bake uncovered in a preheated 350° F. oven for 35 to 40 minutes, or until crispy and cooked. Yield: 4 servings.

TURKEY CUSTARD

This is a good way to use leftover turkey after that Thanksgiving Day* feast. Serve it with a tossed salad and a great dessert. It is a good supper dish.

2 cups chopped cooked turkey
1½ cups soft bread crumbs, or 1 cup stuffing left over from roast turkey
½ teaspoon salt
freshly ground pepper
½ cup grated Cheddar cheese

3 eggs
1½ cups milk
★ ⅔ cup cereal crumbs (cornflakes, Grape-Nuts Flakes, Rice Chex, etc.)
1 tablespoon butter

Grease a 2-quart casserole with butter or margarine. Place half of the turkey in the bottom of the casserole. Top with half of the bread crumbs or stuffing. Sprinkle with salt and pepper if using bread crumbs. If using stuffing do not season. Add half of the cheese. Beat eggs and milk. Pour half over the turkey layer in the casserole. Repeat this process. Sprinkle cereal crumbs on top and dot with butter. Bake in a preheated 350° F. oven for 30 minutes, or until a knife inserted in middle comes out clean. Yield: 4 to 6 servings.

FISH SAUTÉ WITH SHRIMP BUTTER

2 pounds fish fillets (haddock, sole, flounder, etc.)
★ 1½ cups crushed cereal (cornflakes, Total, Grape-Nuts Flakes, Rice Chex, etc.)
¼ cup sesame seeds
2 eggs, beaten with 2 tablespoons water
2 ounces (4 tablespoons) margarine or butter
salt and pepper
Shrimp Butter (recipe follows)

Wipe fish fillets with a damp cloth. Mix cereal crumbs and sesame seeds. Dip fish into egg wash, then roll in crumbs. Heat margarine or butter in a skillet until sizzling. Sauté fish for 5 minutes on each side. Season to taste and serve with shrimp butter. Yield: 4 servings.

Shrimp Butter

4 ounces (½ cup) boiling butter
6 raw shrimps, peeled, cleaned and finely chopped
½ teaspoon salt
freshly ground pepper

Pour boiling butter over shrimps. When shrimps turn pink, add remaining ingredients. If you prefer, you may do this whole process in a blender. Boiling butter will cook the shrimps as they are blended into the sauce. Pour this sauce over the sautéed fish and serve at once. Yield: 4 servings.

FISH TURBANS

Turbans look elegant standing in place on a pretty serving platter. Intersperse them with sprigs of parsley and a wedge of lemon per serving.

1 scallion, chopped
1 small onion, chopped
1 ounce (2 tablespoons) butter
¼ pound mushrooms, chopped
★ 2½ cups crushed cornflakes
salt and pepper

8 fillets of gray sole (flounder
   or haddock may be
   substituted)
2 eggs, beaten with 2
   tablespoons water
oil for deep-frying

Sauté scallion and onion in butter until limp. Add mushrooms and cook for 5 minutes. Stir in ½ cup cornflake crumbs. Season to taste. Divide this stuffing among the 8 fillets. Roll up lengthwise and skewer with a toothpick. Dip rolls into egg wash. Roll in remaining cornflake crumbs. Pour oil into a deep skillet or saucepan to a depth of 2 inches (or use an electric deep-fryer). Heat to sizzling hot (see Note). Drop rolls into fat and fry for 10 minutes. Drain on paper toweling. Serve with Tartar Sauce (p. 75). Yield: 4 servings.

Note: Oil should test 375° to 400° F. on a frying thermometer. If you do not have a thermometer, drop a piece of bread into the oil. If it immediately starts bubbling and sizzling, the oil is ready.

CHEDDAR CHEESE MEAT LOAF

Rather than use the commercial "helpers" on the market, try using rolled oats to stretch your ground beef dishes. This is economical and healthier.

1½ pounds ground beef
1 onion, grated (see Note)
1 garlic clove, crushed
1 teaspoon salt
freshly ground pepper
¾ cup grated Cheddar cheese

★ 1 cup uncooked rolled oats
1 teaspoon dried basil or 1
   tablespoon minced fresh
2 eggs, lightly beaten
1 cup milk

Mix beef with all remaining ingredients. Pat into a loaf pan 9 x 5 x 3 inches. Place in a preheated 350° F. oven and bake for 45 to 50 minutes. Yield: 4 to 6 servings.

Note: Grating onions is a difficult chore. Not only do you weep copiously, but your knuckles also are grated if you don't take care. If you have a blender or food processor, pour the milk into the jar, cut the onion into 4 pieces, and add. Blend or process until onion is puréed.

CHILI PIE

This pie is seasoned with 2 teaspoons chili powder. It may not be enough spice for some. Add as much as you deem fit. Chili is a very personal thing; some like it hot, some do not. The amount I have added is middle of the road.

1 onion, chopped
1 green pepper, seeded and
  chopped
2 tablespoons oil
1 garlic clove, chopped
1½ pounds ground beef

2 teaspoons chili powder
1 teaspoon salt
freshly ground pepper
6 ounces canned tomato paste
1 cup grated Cheddar cheese
★ 1½ cups crushed corn chips

Sauté onion and green pepper in hot oil. Add garlic and sauté for 1 to 2 minutes. Add beef and sauté, mashing beef, until it loses its red color. Add chili powder, salt, pepper to taste, tomato paste and Cheddar cheese. Mix well. Turn into a greased 2-quart casserole. Sprinkle with corn chips. Bake in a preheated 350° F. oven for 25 minutes. Yield: 6 servings.

BREADS AND PANCAKES

BRAN MUFFINS

Here are two different recipes for bran muffins. This one is made with bran flakes, and the next recipe is made with whole bran. Both are very good for the system, adding the natural fiber nutritionists claim we should include in the diet. These muffins freeze well and are very good heated, for breakfast or dinner.

1 cup flour, sifted
½ cup raisins
½ cup chopped nuts
4 teaspoons baking powder
3 tablespoons sugar
dash of salt

¼ teaspoon ground cloves
★ 1¼ cups bran flakes
1½ ounces (3 tablespoons)
  melted margarine
1 egg, lightly beaten
1 cup milk

Sprinkle 3 tablespoons of the flour over the raisins and nuts. Mix well to coat evenly; set aside. Sift remaining flour with baking powder, sugar, salt and cloves. Add bran flakes and mix well. Add margarine, egg and milk to dry mixture; beat well to incorporate. Stir in raisins and nuts. Spoon into 12 well-greased large muffin tins. Bake in a preheated 400° F. oven for 15 to 20 minutes. Yield: 12 muffins.

PINEAPPLE-BRAN MUFFINS

1½ cups flour
1 tablespoon baking powder
¼ cup sugar
1 teaspoon salt
½ teaspoon grated nutmeg
★ 1½ cups All-Bran
1 egg, beaten

½ cup evaporated milk
¼ cup pineapple juice
½ cup crushed pineapple, well
  drained
2 ounces (4 tablespoons)
  melted margarine
1 teaspoon vanilla extract

Sift together flour, baking powder, sugar, salt and nutmeg. Add All-Bran. Combine egg, evaporated milk, pineapple juice and pineapple. Add dry ingredients. Stir in margarine and vanilla. Fill well-greased muffin tins two thirds full. Bake in a preheated 400° F. oven for 25 minutes. Yield: 18 muffins.

MOCK POLENTA

Polenta is made with cornmeal. A similar dish can be made with farina or an uncooked toasted cereal such as Wheatena or Ralston. The procedure is identical, regardless of the grain used. A heavy base is made of the cooked cereal, which is then spread on a plate, cooled, cut into wedges, circles or rectangles, further dressed, sautéed and served as a meat accompaniment.

2 cups water
½ teaspoon salt
★ ¾ cup Cream of Wheat,
    Wheatena or Ralston
2 cups fine dry bread crumbs

1 cup grated Parmesan cheese
2 eggs, beaten with 2
    tablespoons water
¼ pound (½ cup) butter or
    margarine

Heat water with salt to boiling. Gradually stir in cereal. Cook until thick. Pour into a greased shallow dish. Smooth out to a layer about ¼ inch thick. Cool completely. Cut into circles, or rectangles 1 x 2 inches. Mix bread crumbs and cheese. Dip cereal pieces into egg wash. Roll in the mixture of crumbs and cheese. Heat margarine or butter in a skillet. Sauté the coated cereal pieces, turning once. Serve hot as a side dish. Yield: 6 servings.

Variation: Lay sautéed mock polenta in a shallow casserole. Spread with tomato sauce. Sprinkle with grated cheese and bake in a preheated oven (350° F.) for 15 minutes.

CEREAL FLAKE PANCAKES

This recipe was given to me by a friend who had trouble getting her kids to eat eggs. This was her compromise. The children adored these tiny bite-size pancakes.

3 eggs
½ cup milk
★ 2 cups cereal flakes
   (approximately), crushed
   (sweetened or unsweetened)

dash of salt
4 ounces (8 tablespoons)
   margarine or butter
   (approximately)
cinnamon sugar or pancake
   syrup

Beat eggs. Add milk and stir in enough cereal flakes to absorb the egg-milk mixture. Add salt. Allow to rest until cereal flakes soften slightly. Melt 2 tablespoons butter or margarine in a skillet. Drop teaspoons of the cereal batter into skillet. Cook until browned on each side. Repeat until all batter is used. Serve with cinnamon sugar or syrup if using unsweetened cereal. If using sweetened cereal sprinkle with cinnamon only. Yield: 30 pancakes, size of a half dollar.

FRITTATA DOLCE

This dish may remind you of Italian polenta. It is made similarly, using farina rather than cornmeal. It is an excellent accompaniment to meat, chicken or veal dishes. It can also be served in tiny fingers as an appetizer to be nibbled during the cocktail hour.

2 cups milk
★ ½ cup farina or Cream of
   Wheat
½ cup sugar
grated rind of 1 lemon

1 teaspoon almond extract
2 eggs, lightly beaten
★ 1 cup crushed cornflakes
oil

Scald the milk. Slowly stir in farina. Add sugar and lemon rind. Cook, stirring constantly, until thick and smooth. Stir in almond extract. Pour into a greased shallow pan. Cool. Cut into fingers 2 inches long and ⅓ inch wide. Roll in beaten egg, then in crushed cornflakes. Pour oil into a skillet to the depth of 1 inch. Heat to sizzling (see Note, p. 28). Add fritters and deep-fry until golden brown. Remove with a slotted spoon, drain on paper toweling, and serve at once. Yield: approximately 36.

OATMEAL BREAD

3 packages active dry yeast
½ cup tepid water (105° to
  115° F.)
1 tablespoon butter
1 tablespoon bacon fat

½ cup honey
1 cup milk, scalded
1 tablespoon salt
★ 2 cups oatmeal
5½ cups flour

Dissolve yeast in the tepid water. Melt butter, bacon fat and honey in scalded milk. Stir in salt. Pour into a large bowl and cool to tepid. Add oatmeal and dissolved yeast. Stir in flour to make a stiff dough. Turn out on a floured board and knead until smooth and elastic, about 8 minutes. Form into a ball and place in a greased bowl, turning once to grease top. Cover with plastic wrap and place in a warm spot (see Comment, p. 22). Allow dough to rise until doubled in bulk, about 1½ hours.

Punch down, divide into 2 portions, and shape into 2 loaves. Place in 2 greased loaf pans, 4½ x 8 inches. Pans should be no more than half full. Allow to rise until doubled in bulk. Bake in a preheated 375° F. oven for 30 minutes. Cool on a rack. Yield: 2 loaves.

RAISIN-MOLASSES BREAD

★ 3 cups rolled oats
1 tablespoon salt
1 ounce (2 tablespoons)
  margarine, melted
1 cup raisins

4 cups boiling water
1 cup molasses
3 packages active dry yeast
½ cup tepid water (105° to
  115° F.)
6 to 7 cups bread flour

Combine oats, salt, margarine, raisins and boiling water. Add molasses and beat until cool. Sprinkle yeast over tepid water to dissolve it. Stir yeast into oatmeal mixture. Stir in enough flour to make a stiff dough. Turn out onto a floured board and knead until smooth and elastic, about 8 minutes. Place in a greased large bowl, turning once to grease top. Cover with plastic wrap and place in a warm, draft-free spot to rise (see Comment, p. 22) until doubled in bulk.

Punch down, divide into 3 parts, and form into loaves. Place in greased pans 8 x 4½ x 2½ inches and again allow to rise until doubled in bulk. Bake in a preheated 375° F. oven for 40 minutes. Yield: 3 loaves.

SHREDDED-WHEAT BREAD

★ 4 shredded-wheat biscuits
2 cups boiling water
½ cup molasses
½ cup brown sugar
2 tablespoons salt
3 cups milk, scalded

2 packages active dry yeast
½ cup tepid water (105° to
  115° F.)
¼ pound (½ cup) melted
  margarine
6 to 7 cups bread flour

Soak shredded wheat in 2 cups boiling water for 1 hour. Stir molasses, brown sugar and salt into scalded milk. Cool to lukewarm. Sprinkle yeast over tepid water. Mix shredded wheat, milk mixture, yeast and margarine together. Add flour, 1 cup at a time, until you have a stiff dough. Turn out onto a floured board and knead until smooth and elastic. Form into a ball and place in a greased bowl, turning once to grease top. Cover with plastic wrap. Place in a draft-free, warm spot to rise until doubled in bulk (see Comment, p. 22).

Punch down and form into 3 loaves. Place in greased pans 8 x 4½ x 2½ inches and allow to rise until doubled in bulk. Bake in a preheated 375° F. oven for 40 minutes. Cool on a rack. Yield: 3 loaves.

GRAPE-NUTS TEA BREAD

★ ½ cup Grape-Nuts
1 cup sour milk or buttermilk
1 egg, beaten
½ cup sugar
2 cups flour

2 teaspoons baking powder
½ teaspoon salt
½ teaspoon baking soda
½ cup raisins

Combine Grape-Nuts and milk. Allow to soak for 20 minutes. Stir egg and sugar into Grape-Nuts mixture. Sift flour, baking powder, salt and baking soda together twice. Stir into Grape-Nuts mixture. Fold in raisins. Turn into a well-greased loaf pan. Bake in a pre-heated 350° F. oven for 1 hour. Yield: 1 loaf.

DESSERTS MADE FROM CEREALS

DANISH APPLE PUDDING

This is a scrumptious pudding. Serve it while still warm with a large dollop of ice cream.

6 large tart cooking apples
(see Comment)
juice of ½ lemon
½ cup water
1 teaspoon vanilla extract
★ 2 cups crushed cornflakes (or
other nonsweet dry cereal
of your choice)

★ 1 cup uncooked oatmeal
¼ cup packed brown sugar
1 teaspoon ground cinnamon
¾ cup strawberry preserves
(see Note)
¼ pound (½ cup) melted
margarine

Peel, core, and slice apples. Place in a saucepan with lemon juice and ½ cup water. Cook until soft. Add vanilla and set aside. Mix cornflakes, oatmeal, brown sugar and cinnamon. Toss well to incorporate. Grease a 9-inch-square baking dish. Sprinkle with half of the crumb mixture. Spread with cooked apples, then with the strawberry preserves. Top with remaining crumb mixture. Drizzle with melted margarine. Bake in a preheated 350° F. oven for 30 minutes. Serve warm or cooled. Yield: 8 servings.

Note: You may substitute apricot or raspberry preserves for strawberry.

Comment: The best cooking apples are Northern Spy, Rome Beauty, Granny Smith and Greening. Delicious apples are firm and taste fairly good in pies and puddings, but should be well laced with lemon juice to neutralize their bland quality. McIntosh and Cortland are good eating apples, but tend to become mushy when cooked.

Macoun, a new Eastern variety, introduced by Cornell University, is a cross between McIntosh and Jersey Black specifically for both eating and cooking.

FROZEN CUSTARD

Both this custard and the next have the addition of Grape-Nuts. I have found that all males seem to love Grape-Nuts but many females do not. I do not know why. If you have a household of males, as I do, try one of these custards.

1 tablespoon cornstarch	dash of grated nutmeg
⅓ cup sugar	★ 1 cup Grape-Nuts
1½ cups milk, scalded	1 cup heavy cream, whipped
2 eggs, separated	1 teaspoon vanilla extract

Mix cornstarch and sugar. Stir in scalded milk. Cook over hot water, stirring, until thickened, about 5 minutes. Beat egg yolks and very slowly beat in the hot milk mixture. Chill. Stir in nutmeg and Grape-Nuts. Beat egg whites until stiff. Fold egg whites into custard. Fold in whipped cream and vanilla. Pour into a wet 4-cup mold. Freeze until firm. Unmold by wringing a towel out in boiling hot water and draping it over the mold until it releases. Serve with Cocoa Glaze (p. 157). Yield: 8 servings.

GRAPE-NUTS CUSTARD

★ ½ cup Grape-Nuts	⅓ cup sugar
2 cups milk	1 teaspoon vanilla extract
3 eggs	

Soak Grape-Nuts in 2 cups milk for 30 minutes. Beat eggs with sugar and vanilla. Stir in milk mixture. Pour into a 1½-quart baking dish. Set dish in a basin of hot water. Slide the basin into the oven. Bake in a preheated 325° F. oven for 45 minutes, or until a knife inserted in the middle comes out clean. Chill. Yield: 6 servings.

CHOCOLATE OATMEAL SQUARES

½ pound (1 cup) margarine or
butter
2 cups brown sugar
2 eggs
1 teaspoon vanilla extract
2 cups flour, sifted (see p. 159)
1 teaspoon baking soda

dash of salt
★ 2 cups rolled oats
½ cup shelled walnuts,
chopped
6 ounces semisweet chocolate
bits

Cream margarine or butter with brown sugar. Add eggs and vanilla and mix well. Mix flour, baking soda, salt and oats. Blend with egg mixture. Fold in walnuts and chocolate. Pat into a greased 8-inch-square pan. Bake in a preheated 400° F. oven for 15 to 20 minutes. Cool. Cut into bars 1 inch x 2 inches. Yield: 32 bars.

CEREAL CRUST FOR PIES

Before leaving this section on coupons for cereals, let me give you a recipe for crumb crusts. These are the easiest crusts you can make when preparing nonbaked pies.

★ 2 cups crushed cereal crumbs
1 tablespoon sugar

2⅔ ounces (⅓ cup) melted
butter or margarine

Grease a 9-inch pie plate. Mix crumbs, sugar and melted butter or margarine. Press into pie plate. Place in a preheated 350° F. oven for 7 minutes. Cool and fill.

3
COUPONS FOR
SOUPS AND SAUCES

Canned soups are among the most popular items on supermarket shelves. The quality, by and large, is good. Every household has its cache of favorite staples. For a quick and nourishing lunch, nothing beats a good soup and sandwich, or soup and salad. Listed here are numerous ways of combining canned soups for an interesting taste change. As a sauce base for many convenient casseroles, creamed soups are a time-saver. Canned consommés and bouillons are highly recommended for braising, stewing and sauce making. Leftovers may be incorporated in good basic canned soups such as tomato, beef or chicken noodle, or vegetable. Finely chop or grind cold meats and vegetables, add to your soup base with a few fine noodles, a sprinkling of garlic powder, onion salt and Parmesan cheese, and *voilà!* a new and interesting minestrone. Add cooked noodles to thick or creamed soups, but add raw noodles to clear soups. Add ½ cup extra water, when cooking noodles in soup, to replace liquid lost to evaporation and absorption by noodles.

Instant soup bases or bouillon cubes are another must on your staple list. If a recipe calls for stock, the powders and cubes make an acceptable substitute for homemade stock. A word of caution, however: Most soup bases have a high salt content; beware when seasoning your dish. Taste first, add salt later. Several manufacturers offer salt-free bases; I prefer these. Soup-in-a-cup, the latest innovation, does not measure up to canned standards in my estimation; its convenience, however, is undeniable. Shelf accommodation is another consideration: If you have little cupboard space, the packaged soups are easier to store.

I have included packaged sauces in this chapter. Some of these gravies, sauces and garnishes are not too bad; however, I would only use them in a pinch. Gravies fare better than sauces such as béarnaise, hollandaise or Béchamel. The latter suffer from unorthodox preparation. Milk- and egg-based sauces need to be made from scratch in order to maintain their quality. Stock-based gravies lend themselves somewhat better to the instant dehydration process. Tomato-based marinara and other pasta sauces are probably the most successfully packaged items. Do not expect a great sauce from these accommodations. They are a convenience only, and should be considered as such.

Coupons featuring soups or sauces are regularly issued. Make good use of them by consulting the following recipes. The best feature of these items is their long shelf life. Don't be afraid to mix and match. Add several days' leftovers and make what my family calls "must-go" soup, always the most popular of the week, but impossible to repeat. If asked for the recipe, modestly decline, saying there are some secrets you must keep. This chapter includes soup combinations and one bread, vegetable casseroles and main-course dishes.

SOUP COMBINATIONS AND ONE BREAD

INSTANT SENEGALESE SOUP

★ 2 cans (10¾ oz. each)
   condensed cream of chicken
   soup
1½ soup cans milk
2 teaspoons curry powder

½ cup water
1 cup cooked rice
juice of ½ lemon
snipped fresh chives

Combine soup and milk in a saucepan. Mix curry powder with water and stir in. Add rice and simmer for 10 minutes. Chill thoroughly.

Stir in lemon juice. Serve with a sprinkling of chives on top. Yield: 6 servings.

CORN AND BACON CHOWDER

6 slices of bacon, diced
1 onion, chopped
2 potatoes, peeled and
  chopped
2 cups boiling water
16 ounces canned cream-style
  corn

1 quart milk, scalded
1 teaspoon salt
¼ teaspoon pepper
★ 1 can (10¾ oz.) condensed
  New England clam chowder
2 tablespoons chopped
  parsley

Cook bacon in a large pot until crisp. Add onion and cook until limp. Add potatoes and toss well. Add boiling water and cook until potatoes are soft, about 10 minutes. Add corn and scalded milk. Bring to a boil and simmer for 5 minutes. Add salt, pepper and canned soup. Simmer for another 5 minutes. Stir in parsley and serve. Yield: 8 servings.

INSTANT POTAGE SAINT-GERMAIN

★ 1 can (10¾ oz.) condensed
  pea soup
½ soup can tomato juice
1 tablespoon tomato paste
1 cup cream

salt and pepper
½ teaspoon dried basil, or 2
  teaspoons minced fresh
  basil
snipped fresh chives or
  scallions

Place all ingredients except chives or scallions in a saucepan. Bring to a boil, stirring, and heat thoroughly. Serve with a sprinkling of chives or scallions on top. Yield: 4 servings.

INSTANT TOMATO-MUSHROOM BISQUE

1 small onion, chopped
1 tablespoon margarine
1 garlic clove, crushed
★ 1 can (10¾ oz.) condensed
    tomato soup

★ 1 can (10¾ oz.) condensed
    cream of mushroom soup
2 cups milk

Sauté onion in margarine until limp. Add garlic and sauté for 3 minutes more. Stir in soups and milk. Heat, stirring, until hot and smooth. Cook, stirring occasionally, for 10 minutes. Yield: 6 servings.

SUGGESTED CANNED SOUP COMBINATIONS

1. Chicken soup and tomato soup mixed with 1 can milk, 1 can water.
2. Corn chowder and tomato soup mixed with 2 cans skim milk.
3. Cream of mushroom and cream of pea soup, mixed with 2 cans skim milk.
4. Cream of oyster and cream of mushroom soup mixed with 2 cans milk.
5. Tomato and cream of spinach soup mixed with 2 cans water.
6. Vegetable and chicken or turkey noodle soup mixed with 2 cups water.
7. Cream of asparagus and cream of celery mixed with 1 can milk, 1 can water.

Variation: Add a dash of Worcestershire sauce and a pinch of garlic powder to any of the combinations for added zest.

Comment: Powdered, nonfat dry milk may be substituted wherever milk is required. Mix it in proportions according to package instructions. Croutons, grated hard cheese, snipped chives, parsley, paprika and dollops of sour cream make excellent quick garnishes for any of the soup combinations. Add ½ cup fine noodles or rice to the soup, and simmer until tender.

ONION BREAD

1 cup reconstituted nonfat dry milk or whole milk, scalded
2 tablespoons sugar
1½ tablespoons butter or margarine
1 package active dry yeast

¾ cup lukewarm water (105° to 115° F.)
★ 1 envelope (1.38 ozs.) dehydrated onion soup
3½ to 4 cups all-purpose flour
1 egg yolk, beaten with 2 tablespoons water

Mix milk, sugar and butter or margarine. Cool to tepid. Sprinkle yeast over lukewarm water and stir to dissolve (see Note). Add yeast to milk mixture. Stir in soup and enough flour to make a stiff dough. Turn out on a floured board. Knead for 8 minutes, or until dough is smooth and elastic. Place in a greased bowl, turn to grease top, and cover with plastic wrap. Allow dough to rise until doubled in size (see Comment, p. 22).

Punch dough down. Allow to rest for 10 minutes. Shape into 2 loaves. Place in greased bread pans, 8 x 4½ x 2½ inches. Allow to rise again until doubled in size. Brush loaves with egg wash. Bake in a preheated 375° F. oven for 25 minutes. Yield: 2 loaves.

Note: The method of dissolving yeast in lukewarm water before adding to the dough base is called "proofing the yeast."

VEGETABLE CASSEROLES

I seldom use a soup to replace a good sauce in a recipe. However, busy cooks do not always have the time to do things from scratch. If you have time, use 2 cups Béchamel Sauce or Mornay Sauce (see p. 15) in place of the soups suggested.

FAR EAST CELERY

My sister gave me this recipe. It is a delicious way to use up all that celery you don't know what to do with.

4 cups 1-inch pieces of celery
1 can (5 oz.) sliced water chestnuts
1 pimiento, chopped
★ 1 can (10¾ oz.) chicken soup, undiluted

½ cup bread crumbs
¼ cup slivered blanched almonds
1 ounce (2 tablespoons) melted butter

Cook celery in 1 inch of boiling water, covered, for 6 minutes; drain well. Toss celery with water chestnuts, pimiento and undiluted soup. Place in a casserole. Mix bread crumbs, almonds and butter. Sprinkle over top. Bake in a preheated 350° F. oven for 30 minutes. Yield: 6 servings.

Comment: No water or milk is used to dilute the soup due to the high water content in celery. As celery cooks, liquid tends to ooze from the vegetable, naturally diluting the soup. Do not overcook celery, as it should be *al dente* (meaning slightly underdone, or "to the tooth" in Italian).

ASPARAGUS AMANDINE

You may substitute frozen asparagus spears (one 10½-oz. package) when fresh is lacking.

1 pound fresh asparagus
★ 1 can (10½ oz.) cream of
   mushroom soup, undiluted
½ cup milk
½ cup chopped fresh parsley

½ pound mushrooms, sliced
2 ounces (4 tablesoons)
   butter, melted
½ cup bread crumbs
½ cup slivered blanched
   almonds

Wash asparagus spears. Using both hands, bend each spear until it breaks. Retain the upper tender portion. Discard lower portion. Place stalks, standing upright, in a deep narrow pot. Pour in 1 inch of boiling water. Cook, covered, for 6 minutes. Drain well, then cut into 1-inch lengths.

Mix soup, milk and parsley to make a sauce. Sauté mushrooms in 1 ounce of the melted butter. Mix crumbs, almonds, and remaining butter. Arrange half of the asparagus in a buttered 1½-quart casserole. Top with half of the mushrooms and half of the sauce. Repeat. Sprinkle with crumb mixture. Bake in a preheated 350° F. oven for 30 minutes. Yield: 6 to 8 servings.

CAULIFLOWER CHIFFON

Fresh vegetables are so expensive today that any good recipe using frozen vegetables is welcome.

2 packages (10 oz. each)
   frozen cauliflower
2 eggs, separated
★ 1 can (10½ oz.) cream of
   celery soup, undiluted
1 ounce sherry

1 tablespoon cream
½ teaspoon salt
freshly ground pepper
½ cup grated strong Cheddar
   cheese
paprika

Cook cauliflower according to package instructions. Drain well. Arrange in a 1½-quart casserole. Beat egg yolks with soup, sherry, cream, salt, pepper to taste and cheese. Beat egg whites until stiff but not dry. Stir a large tablespoon of egg whites into sauce. Fold in remaining whites. Pour sauce over the cauliflower. Sprinkle with paprika. Bake in a preheated 425° F. oven for 20 minutes. Yield: 6 servings.

MAIN-COURSE DISHES

LASAGNE BOLOGNESE

Dishes originating from the area of Bologna are reputed to be the ultimate in Italian cooking. This recipe adds a new dimension to lasagna, with Mornay sauce taking the place of mozzarella cheese.

½ pound lasagna noodles
1 pound ground beef
1 tablespoon oil
1 garlic clove, chopped
1 teaspoon crumbled dried orégano

★ 1 jar (32 oz.) marinara sauce
1 recipe Mornay Sauce (p. 15)
grated nutmeg
grated Parmesan cheese
1 tablespoon butter

Cook noodles according to package instructions. Drain, rinse well under cold running water, then dry on paper toweling.

Sauté beef in oil until no longer pink, mashing beef with a fork to break up lumps. Add garlic and orégano. Cook for 2 to 3 minutes. Add marinara sauce and stir well to incorporate.

Grease a lasagna dish (see Note) well. Pour a small amount of meat sauce in the bottom of the dish and spread evenly. Cover with a layer of noodles. Add a layer of Mornay sauce and sprinkle with nutmeg. Cover with some of the meat sauce. Repeat until all noodles and sauces are used, ending with meat sauce. Sprinkle generously with Parmesan cheese and dot with the butter. Bake in a preheated 350° F. oven for 30 minutes. Yield: 6 servings.

Note: A baking pan 12 x 9 x 2 inches will do if you do not have a traditional lasagna pan.

BRAISED PORK WITH CAPERS

Loin of pork braised in this fashion is spectacular. It is rich—therefore, it is imperative that all the fat be removed from the pork before proceeding. As the pork is cooked in chicken broth, the meat can well do without a layer of fat to keep it moist. Serve small portions.

6 pounds boneless, trimmed
   loin of pork
oil for browning
1 onion, chopped
1 carrot, chopped
1 garlic clove, chopped
1 teaspoon paprika
★ 1½ cups chicken broth,
   canned or instant

1 teaspoon salt
freshly ground pepper
½ cup dry white wine
3 tablespoons flour
1 cup commercial sour cream,
   at room temperature
½ cup chopped parsley
3 tablespoons drained,
   chopped capers

Brown meat on all sides in oil. Use a Dutch oven with a tight fitting lid that will comfortably accommodate meat. Remove pork from oil and drain on paper toweling. Add onion and carrot to the pot. Cook, stirring, until onion is limp. Add garlic and paprika. Cook, stirring, for 2 to 3 minutes. Add broth, salt, pepper to taste and wine. Bring to a boil on top of stove. Add meat, cover, and place in a preheated 350° F. oven. Bake for 2 hours. Add more broth if meat dries out during braising process. Remove meat. Cover with foil and set aside.

Completely degrease liquid remaining in Dutch oven(see p. 166). Purée liquid in a blender or force through a sieve. Return liquid to the pan. Stir flour into sour cream. Blend well. Beat by the spoonful into puréed liquid. Heat, stirring, then simmer for 15 minutes, stirring often. Stir in parsley and capers. Slice meat, add to sauce, heat and serve. Yield: 10 to 12 servings.

4 COUPONS FOR VEGETABLES

This is a broad category. Canned, frozen and precooked vegetables, such as onion rings and French fried potatoes; potato flakes; noodles and pasta; rice, both instant and processed; dried salad additives; legumes, etc., are some of the items for which coupons are regularly issued. I am including here all those foods that accompany or embellish the main course. Rice, barley, kasha and all grains should technically be in the cereals chapter; however, as they become an integral part of the main course, substituting for a starchy vegetable, they are here considered as "vegetables."

I am a great lover of fresh vegetables; they should be eaten whenever possible. Nevertheless, in winter months, when vegetables are scarce and expensive, we all resort at times to frozen and canned produce. In some cases frozen can be almost as good as fresh. Peas, for instance, are excellent. Chopped broccoli and spinach, used in casseroles, are more than adequate. When making a heavily sauced concoction, it seems unnecessary to use a very expensive fresh vegetable.

Generally speaking, frozen vegetables are better than canned. Do not overcook them; cook for only the length of time indicated on packages. Combinations of vegetables and garnishes with ethnic names are excellent but expensive. Little needs to be done other than heating them in their plastic pouches in boiling water. An extra sprinkling of cheese or an herb of your choice might add to the taste. I have often seen coupons and refunds for these items.

Canned vegetables such as tomato products are staples that must grace most pantry shelves. Other canned vegetables are less satisfactory; the steaming process seems to impair the taste and texture of many vegetables—peas, baked beans and sweet potatoes being exceptions.

In my opinion, this chapter may be the most important in the book. Americans have not been good vegetable cooks in the past. But the interest in health and nutrition has taken this country by storm in the past ten years. It is inevitable that vegetables would come into their own under such an influence. Vegetarianism is being adopted by many households. As inflation takes its toll, more and more people will reduce their meat consumption. Replacing protein when eliminating even one meat meal a week becomes a major problem for the meal planner. Meat supplies 65 percent of the body's protein requirements. Eggs, fish, nuts and grains are the best sources of protein next to meat. Cheese and vegetables follow in close order. This section of the book is designed to help the reader plan well-balanced vegetable courses. I will indicate which dishes can be used in vegetarian diets. Whether or not you have a particular vegetable coupon, I hope you will often refer to this section for creative and nutritious ways of handling vegetables.

CORN FRITTERS

Serve these fritters with Southern Fried Chicken (p. 12).

1 cup sifted flour	★ 1 can (1 lb.) corn kernels,
1 teaspoon baking powder	drained
1 teaspoon salt	2 eggs, separated
	oil for deep-frying

Sift flour, baking powder and salt together into a bowl. Add corn and beaten egg yolks. Beat egg whites until stiff. Fold egg whites into corn mixture. Drop batter by the spoonful into hot oil and fry until browned. Drain on paper toweling. Yield: 8 servings.

CHUCK STEAK CREOLE

Chuck steak is one of the cheapest beef cuts you can buy. Purchase a good meaty piece and trim off as much fat as possible.

1 tablespoon oil
2½ pounds beef chuck steak,
  in one piece
1 green pepper, cut into strips
1 onion, sliced
1 garlic clove, crushed
★ 1 can (16 oz.) plum tomatoes
1 teaspoon salt

freshly ground pepper
bouquet garni (p. 69)
½ cup beef broth, canned or
  fresh
★ 1 jar (1 lb.) small white onions,
  drained and rinsed
1¼ cup chopped parsley

Heat oven to 350° F. Heat oil in a large skillet. Brown meat on both sides. Drain on paper toweling. Add green pepper and onion to skillet. Cook until onion is limp. Add garlic and cook for 1 to 2 minutes. Place beef in a baking dish. Add sautéed vegetables, tomatoes, salt, pepper to taste, *bouquet garni* and broth. Cover and bake for 1¼ hours. Add onions and bake for 15 minutes more. Remove meat and cut into serving portions. Place on a platter. Degrease sauce (see p. 166) and discard *bouquet garni.* Pour sauce over meat. Sprinkle with parsley and serve. Yield: 4 to 5 servings.

DEEP-FRIED ARTICHOKE HEARTS

Vegetables, dipped into batter, then deep-fried, are crisp and flavorful. Italians deep-fry most vegetables, including whole baby artichokes. These are hard to find in most parts of the country so I am recommending frozen artichoke hearts.

★ 2 packages (10 oz. each)
  frozen artichoke hearts
1¼ cups flour
1 teaspoon salt

1 ounce (2 tablespoons)
  melted margarine
3 eggs
1 cup milk
oil for deep-frying

Separate artichoke hearts, but do not defrost. Sift flour and salt into a bowl. Stir in margarine. Beat in eggs and milk. Beat until batter is smooth. Dip artichoke hearts one at a time into the batter. Then immediately drop into oil heated to 375° to 400° F. on a frying thermometer (see Note, p. 28). There should be enough oil to cover vegetable. Fry for 5 to 6 minutes. Serve with roasted or broiled meats. Yield: 6 to 8 servings.

FISH FILLETS WITH POTATO FLAKE COATING

This is an innovative way to use potato flakes. You must purchase the "flake" type of instant potato, rather than the powdered variety, or the coating will not be crispy.

1 egg	★ 1 cup mashed potato flakes
1 tablespoon lemon juice	2 tablespoons sesame seeds
1 teaspoon salt	1 ounce (2 tablespoons) butter
freshly ground pepper	or margarine
2 pounds fish fillets of your	¼ cup white wine
choice	4 lemon wedges

Beat egg with lemon juice, salt and pepper to taste. Dip fish fillets into this mixture. Mix potato flakes and sesame seeds. Roll fillets in potato mixture. Heat butter or margarine in a skillet. Quickly brown fish fillets on both sides. Remove from pan and keep warm. Add wine to pan and cook until almost evaporated. Pour the deglazing liquid over fish. Serve with lemon wedges. Yield: 4 servings.

LASAGNE WITH BÉCHAMEL SAUCE

Eliminate the chicken and this makes a great vegetarian supper. Serve with a huge tossed salad and light dessert.

★ 1 pound lasagna noodles
½ Spanish onion, sliced
¼ cup olive oil
2 tomatoes, peeled, seeded and chopped
★ 1 can (1 lb.) Italian plum tomatoes, drained and forced through a food mill or blender
1 garlic clove, chopped
½ teaspoon crumbled dried orégano
½ teaspoon dried or 1½ teaspoons minced fresh basil

1 teaspoon salt
freshly ground pepper
3 cups Béchamel Sauce (p. 15)
¼ cup dry vermouth
★ 1 package (10 oz.) frozen chopped spinach
1 pound mushrooms, sliced
1 ounce (2 tablespoons) butter
2 cups chopped cooked chicken
½ cup grated Parmesan cheese
1 pound cottage cheese

Cook lasagna according to package instructions. Drain well and rinse in cold water. Dry on paper towels. Sauté onion in oil until limp but not browned. Remove half of the onion and set aside. Add fresh tomatoes to the onion and cook for 10 minutes. Add puréed canned tomatoes, garlic, orégano, basil, salt and pepper to taste. Cover and simmer for 1 hour. Set the tomato sauce side.

Mix Béchamel sauce with remaining onion and the vermouth. Oil a lasagna pan. Cook and drain the spinach. Sauté the mushrooms in the butter until tender. Lay one layer of noodles in the bottom of the pan. Top with a layer of some of the spinach, mushrooms and chicken. Top with Béchamel sauce and a sprinkling of Parmesan; dot with cottage cheese. Pour a layer of tomato sauce over all. Repeat until all ingredients are used, ending with tomato sauce. Liberally sprinkle with Parmesan cheese. Bake in a preheated 400° F. oven for 30 minutes. Yield: 8 to 10 servings.

HONEYED SWEET POTATOES

This is a variation on candied sweet potatoes.

★ 1 can (16 oz.) sweet potatoes,
    well-drained
salt and freshly ground pepper
1 ounce (2 tablespoons) butter
    or margarine

¼ cup honey
¼ cup orange juice
paprika

Lay potatoes in a shallow baking dish. Sprinkle with salt and pepper to taste. Heat next 3 ingredients and pour over vegetable. Bake in a preheated 400° oven for 20 minutes. Sprinkle with paprika before serving. Yield: 4 servings.

TAGLIATELLE VERDI

This can be served as a vegetarian dish if the prosciutto is eliminated.

★ 1 package (10 oz.) frozen peas
1 teaspoon sugar
★ 1 pound green noodles
8 cups boiling water, with 1
    teaspoon salt added
2 ounces (4 tablespoons)
    butter

salt and pepper
½ cup heavy cream
2 egg yolks
1 cup julienne strips of
    prosciutto
½ cup grated Parmesan
    cheese

Cook peas according to package instructions with 1 teaspoon of sugar added to the water. Cook noddles in boiling water until just barely tender. Drain well, then rinse in cold water. Heat butter in a large saucepan. Add noodles and sauté them, tossing constantly for 5 minutes. Season to taste. Mix cream and egg yolks. Off the heat, stir into the hot noodles. Add prosciutto. Return to *very* low heat and stir until sauce begins to thicken. *Do not boil,* or eggs will curdle. Add peas and sprinkle with cheese. Yield: 8 servings.

MASHED POTATO TART

This delicious potato dish is great to make when there are leftover mashed potatoes. However, I find leftover fresh potatoes discolor and have a stale unattractive flavor. The instant flakes do not discolor and don't have that tacky taste. This is one time when the processed product works better than leftovers.

pastry for 1-crust, 9-inch deep pie (pp. 89 and 93)
★ 1 package (10 oz.) frozen chopped spinach
★ 2 cups mashed potatoes, made from instant flakes according to package instructions
1 medium-size onion, chopped
¼ pound mushrooms, sliced
2 ounces (4 tablespoons) butter
1 garlic clove, chopped
10 tablespoons grated Parmesan cheese
½ cup heavy cream
1 egg
1 teaspoon salt
freshly ground pepper

Line a deep pie plate (6-cup capacity) with the pastry, allowing a 1-inch overhang. Cook spinach and drain very well. Mix spinach and mashed potatoes. Sauté onion and mushrooms in butter for 5 minutes. Add garlic and sauté for 1 to 2 minutes more. Scrape into potato-spinach mixture. Add 8 tablespoons of the cheese, the cream, egg, salt and pepper to taste. Turn into prepared pastry shell. Fold up the 1-inch overhang over filling, leaving the center of pie exposed. Sprinkle with remaining 2 tablespoons cheese. Place in a preheated 375° F. oven and bake for 4 to 5 minutes. Yield: 8 to 10 servings.

RICE PILAF

Cooked chicken, seafood or meat may be added to this to make a heartier supper dish, if so desired. Any ordinary, natural white rice, short or long grain, but not instant may be used.

1 onion, chopped
1½ ounces (3 tablespoons),
   butter or margarine
★ 1½ cups white rice

3 cups chicken or beef broth,
   canned or instant
bouquet garni (p. 69)
1 teaspoon salt
freshly ground pepper

Sauté onion in butter or margarine in a heavy-bottomed casserole with a tight-fitting lid (see Note 1). Add rice and cook, stirring constantly (see Note 2), for 5 minutes. Pour in broth, add *bouquet garni,* salt and pepper to taste. Bring to a boil on top of the stove. Cover tightly. Place in a preheated 350° F. oven and bake for 20 minutes, or until all liquid has been absorbed. Remove and discard *bouquet garni.* Fluff with a fork and serve. Yield: 8 servings.

Note 1: A heavy-bottomed casserole, stove-to-oven, is a necessity for cooking rice. Enameled cast iron is a good choice. The weight of the pot distributes the heat slowly and evenly throughout the dish.

Note 2: This initial cooking of dry rice evenly distributes the onion and fat and also precooks the starch in the rice, resulting in a fluffy light texture.

OKRA CREOLE

1 onion, sliced
1½ ounces (3 tablespoons),
   butter or margarine
1 green pepper, sliced
★ 1 package (10 oz.) frozen okra

2 tomatoes, peeled and
   chopped
1 teaspoon salt
freshly ground pepper
3 tablespoons chopped
   parsley

Sauté onion in butter or margarine until limp. Add green pepper and cook for 5 minutes. Add okra and tomatoes. Season to taste. Cook over very low heat, covered, for 10 minutes. Sprinkle with parsley. Yield: 4 servings.

SPANAKOPITA

This Greek spinach-cheese pie is fine for a vegetarian supper or luncheon dish. Serve with a Greek salad and light dessert—delicious!

¼ cup olive oil
1 small onion, chopped
3 scallions, chopped
1 garlic clove, crushed
★ 2 packages (10 oz. each),
    frozen chopped spinach,
    defrosted and drained
½ cup chopped fresh dill, or 2
    tablespoons dried dill

¼ cup chopped parsley
½ teaspoon salt
freshly ground pepper
⅓ cup milk
½ pound feta cheese,
    crumbled
4 eggs
½ pound (1 cup), butter or
    margarine, melted
½ pound fillo dough (see
    Note)

Heat oil in a small skillet. Add onion and scallions; sauté until limp. Add garlic and sauté for 1 minute. Press as much liquid as possible from spinach, and place in a large bowl. Scrape in onions, scallions and garlic. Add dill, parsley, salt, pepper to taste, milk and crumbled cheese. Mix well. Beat in the eggs one at a time.

Brush with butter a baking pan 12 x 7 x 2 inches. Line with 1 sheet of fillo dough. Brush dough with melted butter. Repeat this process 7 times, using 8 layers of fillo. Spread with spinach mixture. Top with another 8 layers of fillo dough, each brushed with butter. Trim excess dough from sides of pie. Bake in a preheated 350° F. oven for 45 minutes, or until pastry is browned and crisp. Cut into squares. Yield: 8 servings.

Note: Fillo or phyllo dough can be purchased in specialty shops and some supermarkets in 1-pound packages, containing 32 sheets. Sheets should be approximately 14 x 18 inches in size, but may vary according to manufacturer. Wrap unused fillo dough in plastic wrap immediately after opening. Overwrap with foil or freezer wrap and store in the refrigerator, or freeze for longer storage. Fillo dough, unopened, will keep in the refrigerator for 5 weeks.

5 COUPONS FOR MEATS, FISH AND POULTRY

In this chapter I have grouped all meat, poultry and fish products for which coupons are regularly issued. This includes canned, frozen and fresh items. Occasionally a coupon is issued for such foods as turkey breast, Cornish hens and fish, under a given company label. I have rarely seen coupons for fresh meats. Most supermarkets have their own meats or use a specific meat supplier unknown to the general public. These supermarkets do advertise meat sales in their weekly publications, but coupons *per se* are not common.

Many of the large frozen food houses issue coupons when introducing a new item, or when running a special on fish and poultry. Cured foods such as frankfurters, ham and bacon often have coupons issued toward their purchase. You will find these coupons can be used in making hors-d'oeuvre and main dishes based on fish and on meat and poultry.

APPETIZERS

CRAB-MEAT PUFFS

You can replace the crab meat with any seafood of your choice; even tuna will do in a pinch.

1 recipe Pâte à Chou (p. 158)
1 cup Mornay Sauce (p. 15)
★ 1 can (6½ oz.) crab meat, drained and flaked

1 tablespoon capers, chopped
¼ teaspoon dry mustard

Make tiny cream puffs, using a teaspoon to drop batter on a cookie sheet. Bake as directed. Make a fairly thick Mornay sauce. Mix sauce with crab meat, then add capers and mustard. Remove caps from puffs and fill with crab mixture. Place filled puffs in a 350° F. oven for 5 minutes to heat, then serve at once. Yield: 24 puffs.

Microwave Cooking: Heat on "high" setting for 2 minutes.

PÂTÉ CIGARETTES

If you can afford *pâté de foie gras* for this recipe, it will be even better, but canned liver pâté makes a good dish.

★ 1 can (4 oz.) liver pâté
¼ pound (½ cup) sweet butter, softened
★ 16 very thin (3 x 5 inch) slices of boiled ham

1 tablespoon prepared Dijon mustard
½ cup chopped fresh parsley

Mix liver pâté with half of the butter. Mash well to incorporate. Divide equally among slices of ham and spread the mixture to cover each slice. Roll up ham slices and cut each into 2 pieces. Mix remaining butter with mustard. Spread on ends of ham rolls, then dip ends into parsley. Chill before serving. Yield: 32 pieces.

FRANKFURTERS IN BATTER

These little franks can be made ahead and reheated in the oven, but they taste better when fresh.

1 egg	½ teaspoon dry mustard
½ cup milk	½ tablespoon chili powder
1 cup flour	★ 1 pound miniature frankfurters
1 teaspoon baking powder	oil for deep-frying
2 tablespoons cornmeal	prepared Dijon mustard

Combine egg and milk. Beat in next 5 ingredients to make a batter. Allow to stand for at least 20 minutes. Dip frankfurters into batter. Heat 2 inches of oil to sizzling hot, 375° F. on a frying thermometer (see Note, p. 28). Place a metal colander in the hot oil. Drop frankfurters into oil and cook for 2 to 3 minutes. Lift colander from oil and drain frankfurters. Repeat until all frankfurters are cooked. Serve hot with Dijon mustard. Yield: 6 to 8 servings.

MAIN-COURSE DISHES— FISH

SALMON CROQUETTES

1 cup medium-thick Béchamel
   Sauce (p. 15)
★ 1 can (1 lb.) salmon, bones
   removed and drained
1 teaspoon salt
freshly ground pepper
½ teaspoon prepared mustard
1 cup soft bread crumbs

flour for dredging
1 egg, beaten with 2
   tablespoons water
1½ cups fine dry bread
   crumbs
⅓ cup margarine or butter
Tartar Sauce (p. 75)

Mix Béchamel sauce with salmon, salt, pepper to taste, mustard and soft bread crumbs. Mix well and form into croquettes. Dredge with flour. Dip into egg wash. Roll in dry bread crumbs. Chill for several hours. Melt butter or margarine in a large skillet. When sizzling hot, brown croquettes on all sides. Serve with tartar sauce. Yield: 8 croquettes.

Note: Croquettes are traditionally shaped like little cones; however, it is acceptable to shape them in rolls or patties, if so desired.

Microwave Cooking: Prepare croquettes well ahead of time. Heat in oven on "high" setting for 3 minutes just before serving.

CRAB CASSEROLE

3 cups medium-thick
   Béchamel Sauce (p. 15)
★ 2 cans (6½ oz. each) crab
   meat, drained
½ pound mushrooms, sliced
2½ ounces (5 tablespoons)
   butter or margarine, melted

½ cup chopped scallions
2 pimientos, drained and diced
4 eggs, hard-cooked and sliced
2 ounces sherry
½ cup grated Parmesan
   cheese
½ cup fine dry bread crumbs

Mix Béchamel sauce with crab meat. Sauté mushrooms in 1½ ounces (3 tablespoons) butter or margarine for 5 minutes. Add scallions and cook for 3 minutes. Scrape into crab mixture along with pimientos, eggs and sherry. Turn into a buttered 2-quart casserole. Mix cheese and crumbs with remaining butter and toss well. Sprinkle crumb mixture on top of casserole. Place in a preheated 350° F. oven and bake for 35 to 40 minutes, or until bubbly hot and browned on top. Yield: 8 servings.

Microwave Cooking: Sprinkle prepared casserole liberally with paprika. Place in oven on "high" setting and cook for 15 minutes.

FISH STICK CASSEROLE FLORENTINE

This is an easy way to make a busy-day dinner with a minimum of fuss.

★ 2 packages (9 oz. each)
  breaded fish sticks
2 packages (10 oz. each)
  frozen chopped spinach
1 onion, chopped

1 ounce (2 tablespoons) butter
  or margarine
¼ pound mushrooms, sliced
1 recipe Mornay Sauce (p. 15)
¼ cup grated Cheddar or
  Parmesan cheese

Using an accommodating baking dish, lay fish sticks from 1 package, side by side, in the bottom. Cook spinach according to package instructions. Drain very well. Sauté onion in butter until limp. Add mushrooms and sauté for 2 to 3 minutes. Scatter the spinach and sautéed vegetables over the fish. Pour half of the Mornay sauce over top. Lay remaining fish sticks over top of vegetables and sauce. Top with remaining sauce. Sprinkle with cheese. Bake in a preheated 350° F. oven for 25 minutes, or until bubbly hot. Yield: 6 servings.

Comment: Whenever you see the term "Florentine," it means that spinach is part of the dish.

Microwave Cooking: Be sure you use a glass, plastic or ceramic dish. Bake on "high" setting for 15 minutes, or until bubbling hot.

CIOPPINO

This is a soup-stew. It is San Francisco's version of *bouillabaisse*. Serve it as a supper dish with garlic bread and a tossed salad.

1 pound mussels or clams, in the shell
1 tablespoon margarine
1 large onion, chopped
1 garlic clove, crushed
1 teaspoon dried basil, or 1 tablespoon minced fresh
1 teaspoon dried and crumbled orégano
1 can (1 lb.) tomatoes, drained and crushed

1 quart good fish stock or clam juice (see Comment)
¾ cup dry red wine
1 teaspoon salt (see Note)
freshly ground pepper
★ 1 pound shrimp, shelled and deveined
★ 1 pound Dungeness or Alaska crab, shelled
2 pounds fish filets
★ 1 can (7 oz.) chopped clams

Scrub mussels or clams; remove beards from mussels. Soak either shellfish in salted water until you are ready to use them. Heat margarine in a large pot. Sauté onion until limp. Add garlic and cook for 2 minutes. Add herbs and cook for 1 minute, stirring. Add tomatoes, fish stock, wine, salt and pepper to taste. Simmer for 30 minutes. Add clams or mussels, shrimp, crab meat, fish (cut in chunks). Cook for 5 minutes. Discard any clams or mussels that have not opened completely. Add canned clams just before serving. Yield: 12 to 15 servings.

Note: If using clam juice, taste before adding salt. Bottled clam juice can be very salty.

Comment: Making your own fish stock is very economical. Most fishmongers will give you heads, bones and fins for free. Cover these with water in a large pot. Add 1 onion, 1 bay leaf, 1 carrot and a celery rib, leaves and all, a sprig of parsley, 1 tablespoon salt and a few peppercorns. Bring to a boil, cover and simmer for 30 minutes, no more. Fish loses its quality if cooked longer than 30 minutes. Strain. Freeze in 2-cup plastic measures. Run under hot water to release the solid chunk of fish stock. Place these chunks in a plastic bag, labeled, in the freezer. You always have fish stock on hand for soups and sauces.

LOBSTER WITH MELON, AU GRATIN

This delicious dish is expensive; however, occasionally a coupon may be issued for frozen rock lobster tails. If so, rush to avail your-self of this, and serve the dish the next time you want to impress someone.

★ 3 packages (8 oz. each) frozen rock lobster tails
1 cup medium-thick Mornay Sauce (p. 15)
1 small onion, chopped
2 ounces (4 tablespoons) butter, melted
1 garlic clove, crushed
1 teaspoon curry powder

1 cup soft bread crumbs
2 ounces sherry
1 cup finely chopped honeydew melon
1 cup fine dry bread crumbs
½ cup grated Parmesan cheese
2 tablespoons chopped fresh parsley

Drop frozen lobster tails into salted boiling water and cook until meat is firm, 2 to 3 minutes. Remove from water and drain well. Cool. Carefully remove meat from tails, reserving shells. Chop meat finely and add to Mornay sauce. Sauté onion in 1 ounce (2 table-spoons) of butter. Add garlic and curry powder. Sauté for 3 minutes. Scrape into lobster mixture. Stir in soft bread crumbs and sherry. Mix well to incorporate. Fold in chopped melon. Pile this mixture into reserved lobster shells (see Note). Mix dry bread crumbs, cheese, remaining butter and parsley. Sprinkle over top. Bake in a preheated 350° F. oven for 15 to 20 minutes, or until hot. Yield: 4 servings.

Note: If the lobster tails are very small, I suggest that the final mix-ture be piled onto large scallop shells (sold in most good house-wares departments). Proceed with the recipe as designated.

MAIN COURSE DISHES— MEAT AND POULTRY

APRICOT-GLAZED ROCK CORNISH HENS

If you see coupons for Rock Cornish hens, take full advantage of this offer. These little birds are great to have on hand for special occasions. I prefer 1 pound birds. If you have 2 pound birds, then be prepared to serve a half bird per person.

★ 4 Rock Cornish hens, 1 pound each
½ cup chopped mushrooms
3 ounces (6 tablespoons) butter
2 cups cooked brown rice
½ cup chopped dried apricots

½ cup chopped fresh parsley
1 teaspoon salt
freshly ground pepper
1 cup apricot preserves
2 ounces sherry

Wash hens and pat dry. Sauté mushrooms in 1 ounce (2 tablespoons) butter until tender. Mix rice, apricots, parsley, salt, pepper to taste and mushrooms. Toss to blend well. Stuff the hen cavities with this mixture. Skewer cavities closed with toothpicks. Wrap a small piece of aluminum foil around the end of each drumstick, just reaching above where meat starts (see Note). Tie the legs together just under breast bone. Tie the wing joints together, running the string under the bird. Smear each bird with 1 tablespoon of soft margarine. Salt and pepper liberally. Place in a preheated 350° F. oven and bake for 30 minutes.

Meanwhile, place apricot preserves in a small saucepan. Add sherry and heat over low heat until preserves melt. Brush hens with this glaze. Bake for another 45 minutes, brushing every 15 minutes with the glaze. Remove aluminum foil cuffs. Cut strings and remove. Serve at once. Yield: 4 servings.

Note: The aluminum cuff prevents the meat from shrinking away from the bone and exposing a long, angular, unattractive joint.

CUBAN ROAST

Sausage is used in conjunction with beef in many provincial dishes. Each country has its own specialty.

★ ½ pound chorizo or kielbasa
(see Note)
4 pounds beef rump or eye-
round roast
salt and pepper
2 tablespoons oil
1 large onion, chopped
¾ cup chopped carrots
3 garlic cloves, chopped

2 tablespoons chili powder
1 tablespoon crumbled dried
orégano
2 cups canned tomatoes,
crushed
2 tablespoons tomato paste
1 cup beef broth, canned or
instant

Cut sausage lengthwise into quarters to match the size of roast. Remove all casings. Force holes into the center of the meat with a sharp knife, turning the knife while still in the meat to make a hole big enough to insert the long pieces of sausage. Force sausage into holes in meat. Tie meat if necessary. Salt and pepper liberally. Heat oil in a Dutch oven. Brown meat on all sides. Remove from pan and drain on paper toweling. Add vegetables to pan. Sauté until onion is limp. Stir in chili powder and orégano. Cook, stirring, for 2 to 3 minutes. Add tomatoes, tomato paste and beef broth. Return meat to pan. Bring to a boil on top of stove. Cover. Place in a preheated 350° F. oven and bake for 2½ hours. Remove meat from pan liquids. Slice meat and keep warm. Strain juices into a saucepan. Remove as much grease as possible from the juices. Bring liquid to a boil and reduce over high heat to about 1½ cups, then pour over meat. Yield: 8 servings.

Note: Chorizo is a hot Spanish or Mexican sausage available wherever there are Latin-speaking Americans. Kielbasa is a Polish sausage, available throughout the United States, and a good substitute. Coupons are often issued for kielbasa.

CASSOULET

This French dish from the Languedoc requires much assembly and many hours of baking. It is a distant cousin of our Boston baked beans and can be prepared many days ahead, to be frozen and rebaked before serving. It makes an excellent meal-in-one buffet presentation, accompanied by a huge tossed salad and hot French bread.

1 pound dried navy beans
salt
★ 1 duckling
freshly ground pepper
1 pound boneless pork, cubed
1 pound boneless lamb, cubed
flour for dredging (see Note 2)
★ 1 pound garlic or Polish
sausage, cut into 1-inch
pieces
2 large onions, chopped

2 garlic cloves, chopped
4 tomatoes, peeled, seeded
and chopped
2 celery ribs, chopped
1 cup white wine
3 cups beef broth
¼ pound salt pork, chopped
1 teaspoon dry mustard
bouquet garni (p. 69)
3 cups soft bread crumbs
½ cup chopped fresh parsley

Soak beans in water to cover overnight. Drain, cover again with water, add 1 teaspoon salt and simmer, covered, until barely tender. Drain and set aside. Wash the cavity of the duckling. Salt and pepper cavity liberally. Prick duckling all over surface with a sharp-tined fork. Place the bird on a rack in a deep baking dish (see Comment). Roast uncovered in a preheated 350° F. oven for 1½ to 2 hours until skin is crispy and dry. Cool, cut into small portions and set aside. Pour 3 tablespoons of duck fat into a very large skillet.

Dredge (see Note 1) pork and lamb with flour. Shake off excess flour. Brown meats, a bit at a time, in the duck fat in a very large skillet. Drain on paper toweling. Set meats aside. Sauté sausage in the same skillet for 5 to 6 minutes. Drain on paper toweling and set aside.

Add half of the onions to the same skillet and sauté until limp. Add 1 garlic clove, half of the tomatoes and half of the celery. Sauté for 2 to 3 minutes. Return meats to the skillet. Add wine to the broth and stir to a mix. Pour half of this liquid mixture over the meats.

Bring to a boil, reduce heat and simmer, covered, for 1 hour. Set aside.

Sauté salt pork in a heavy-bottomed large stovetop-to-oven casserole. When enough fat has been rendered from salt pork, add remaining onion and sauté until limp. Add 1 garlic clove, remaining tomatoes and celery and the dry mustard. Sauté for 5 minutes. Add precooked beans and remaining wine-broth mixture. Bring to a boil on top of stove. Add 1 teaspoon salt, ½ teaspoon pepper and the *bouquet garni.* Cover tightly. Place in a preheated 300° F. oven and bake for 45 minutes.

Assembly of Cassoulet: The procedure to this point may be done well in advance of serving, the cassoulet to be assembled and baked on the day of service.

In a large earthenware casserole (see Note 2), place a layer of the beans and their liquid. Cover with one quarter of the sausage, duck and meats. Repeat 3 times, ending with beans. Add enough liquid from both beans and meat to cover. Reserve remaining liquids to add if cassoulet dries out during baking. Cover the top with a thick layer of bread crumbs. Place casserole in a preheated 300° F. oven and bake for 1 hour. Stir crust down into cassoulet. Add more liquid if necessary. Cover with another thick layer of bread crumbs. Bake for 20 minutes. Stir crust down into cassoulet. Repeat the last process twice more. After the final layering of bread crumbs, bake but do not stir crust down into cassoulet. Remove from oven and allow cassoulet to rest for 10 minutes. Sprinkle with parsley and serve. Yield: 10 to 12 very hearty servings.

Note 1: The most efficient way to "dredge" anything is to place the flour, seasoned or unseasoned, or fine crumbs, in a plastic bag. Add the food product to the bag, a small amount at a time, and shake vigorously until well coated. Repeat until all is dredged.

Note 2: An earthenware vessel is traditional for long, slow cooking in an oven. Boston baked beans were cooked in an earthenware bean pot and the French used a *cassole d'Issel,* a specialized form of earthenware pot, to do their cassoulets. An enameled cast-iron or stoneware pot will work just as well.

Comment: Use a deep roasting pan when baking a duck. Fat in a duck is so excessive that a shallow pan could possibly overflow and the fat could burn in the oven. Duck fat is considered by the French to be the best fat for sautéing meat and vegetables when making ragouts and stews. It keeps well in the refrigerator and adds a subtle taste to your final product.

Microwave Cooking: Both the initial braising of the beans and meats can be done in the microwave oven. After sautéing the meats and vegetables, scrape them into a plastic, glass or ceramic bowl. Add meats and broth-wine combination. Cover with waxed paper and cook on "high" setting for 30 minutes. Do the same with the beans and cook on "high" setting for 20 to 25 minutes. After assembling the casserole in a ceramic or earthenware casserole, place in the microwave on "high" setting. Rotate every 10 minutes. Bake for 30 minutes. Press crust down into cassoulet. Recrumb top. Bake for 8 to 10 minutes and again press crust down into cassoulet. Bake for 10 minutes longer. Repeat once more. Bake until crumbs are crusty. Sprinkle with parsley and serve.

SAUSAGE-STUFFED POT ROAST

Another sausage-beef dish, tasty and hearty. Good cold weather fare. Try it when your supermarket runs a special on beef for pot roast.

4 pounds rolled beef chuck or blade roast	1 teaspoon salt
★ 1 pound pepperoni sausage	freshly ground pepper
2 tablespoons oil	¼ cup cider vinegar
1 onion, chopped	1 tablespoon brown sugar
1 garlic clove, chopped	1 leafy celery sprig
1 carrot, chopped	1 parsley sprig
2 cups beef bouillon, canned or instant	1 bay leaf

Untie the roast and lay it out flat. Remove casing from sausage and place sausage down center of roast. Re-tie roast. Heat oil in a large roasting pan with a lid. Brown meat on all sides. Remove from heat and set aside. Add onion, garlic and carrot to fat in pan. Sauté 5 minutes. Pour bouillon over all. Add salt, pepper to taste, vinegar and brown sugar. Tie celery, parsley and bay leaf together with a string (see Note). Lay on top of vegetables. Bring bouillon to a boil on top of stove. Add meat. Cover. Place in a preheated 325° F. oven and braise for 2 to 2½ hours. Remove meat from juices. Discard *bouquet garni*. Skim off as much fat as possible (see Note, p. 166). Bring juices to boil on top of stove. Reduce over high heat by half. If you prefer a thicker sauce see Comment. Serve sauce with sliced meat. Yield: 8 servings.

Note: Parsley sprig, celery leaves and bay leaf tied together is known as a *bouquet garni*.

Comment: The French have a way of thickening hot liquids. They mix equal portions of butter and flour and knead into a paste. The paste is then rolled into 1-inch balls. These little balls are dropped into the boiling liquid and the liquid is whisked until the required thickness is reached. These little balls are called *beurre manié*.

STUFFED FRANKFURTERS

This is a quick way to dress up a frankfurter. Use potato flakes to make the mashed potatoes if you are in a desperate rush, and voila—instant dinner.

4 cups mashed potatoes
salt and pepper
1 ounce (2 tablespoons),
   butter or margarine

★ 8 skinless frankfurters
prepared Dijon mustard
8 thin slices of mild Cheddar
   cheese
chopped fresh parsley

Mix mashed potatoes with salt and pepper to taste and butter or margarine. Boil frankfurters in water for 8 minutes. Preheat broiler. Drain frankfurters and slash down the middle. Spread each one with mustard. Pile potatoes on top of each slash. Top with cheese. Broil for several minutes, or until cheese melts. Sprinkle with parsley and serve. Yield: 4 servings.

SCOTCH EGGS

This is a dish reminiscent of my Scottish-Canadian background. These eggs can be great as a brunch dish, easily prepared well ahead, refrigerated and baked just before serving.

★ ½ pound bulk pork sausage
   meat
½ pound lean ground beef
★ 6 strips of bacon, cooked and
   crumbled
1 teaspoon Worcestershire
   sauce

½ teaspoon salt
freshly ground pepper
¼ cup milk
6 hard-cooked eggs, shelled
1 raw egg
2 tablespoons water
1 cup fine dry bread crumbs

Mix sausage meat, ground beef, bacon, Worcestershire sauce, salt, pepper to taste and milk. Blend well and divide into 6 portions. Pat each portion around a hard-cooked egg. Beat raw egg with 2 tablespoons water. Dip meat-egg packages into egg wash, then roll in bread crumbs. Arrange eggs in a single layer in a shallow baking dish. Bake in a preheated 400° F. oven for 35 minutes. Yield: 6 servings.

STUFFED PORK TENDERLOINS WITH GINGER SAUCE

This is a delicious and unusual dish. Pork tenderloins are the best part of the pig. Ask your butcher for them; a supermarket seldom has them in stock.

2 pork tenderloins, 2 pounds
   each
salt and freshly ground pepper
¼ pound pitted prunes
2 apples, peeled, seeded and
   chopped

★ ½ pound sweet Italian
   sausage, or sausage of your
   choice
★ 4 slices of bacon
   Ginger Sauce (recipe follows)

Slice tenderloins lengthwise down the middle, almost but not quite through. Open flat, cover with waxed paper, and pound with a mallet until each tenderloin is flattened. Salt and pepper liberally. Chop prunes and place half of prunes on top of one tenderloin. Top with half of chopped apples. Cut ends off 3 or 4 sausages. Lay sausages down middle of tenderloin with ends pushed together, forming one long sausage. Top with remaining prunes and apples. Lay second tenderloin over the stuffing. Tie together, overlapping edges. Cover with slices of bacon. Bake in a preheated 325° F. oven for 1½ to 2 hours. Cut and remove strings. Serve with ginger sauce. Yield: 8 servings.

Ginger Sauce

1½ cups pear juice (see Note)
juice of ½ lemon
1 tablespoon grated fresh
   gingerroot

1 tablespoon cornstarch
¼ cup cold water or pear juice

Heat pear juice in a small saucepan. Add lemon juice and ginger-root. Mix cornstarch with cold water or pear juice. Stir into hot sauce. Cook until sauce is thick and clear.

Note: Drain the juice from a large can of pears. Use the pears for another dessert.

Comment: You will notice that I have various ways of thickening sauces. If the sauce is prepared ahead, it is made with a *roux* (see Note, Béchamel Sauce, p. 15) and added boiling liquid. If braising liquids are to be thickened, they are either reduced over high heat or *beurre manié* (see Comment, p. 69) is beaten into the boiling liquid. If the sauce is made with fruit juices and condiments, it is thickened with cornstarch or arrowroot. These starches thicken the liquids without making the sauce opaque, so that the natural color of the fruit juice is retained; this is most attractive when pieces of the fruits are added to the sauce.

TURKEY PICCATA

I have seen coupons for uncooked whole turkey breasts. This recipe can be prepared with chicken or turkey breasts. Have your butcher bone the breast, cut into ½-inch slices, then flatten slightly between sheets of waxed paper. This gives a thin layer of meat like veal scaloppine (see Note). This recipe was originally made with veal scaloppine; with veal so expensive, turkey makes an elegant substitute.

3 pounds turkey breast cut
 into 6 even slices
  or
3 pounds boned chicken
 breasts
2 cups soft bread crumbs
¾ cup grated Parmesan
 cheese

1 teaspoon garlic powder
1 teaspoon salt
freshly ground pepper
½ cup chopped fresh parsley
4 ounces (½ cup) melted
 margarine
Lemon Butter (recipe
 follows)
6 thin slices of lemon

If your butcher has not flattened the slices, do it yourself. Cut each flattened piece into halves. Mix crumbs, cheese, garlic powder, salt, pepper to taste and parsley. Dip meat into melted margarine, then roll in crumbs. Lay in a single layer in a shallow baking dish. Place in a preheated 350° F. oven and bake for 15 minutes. Remove to a heated serving plate. Pour lemon butter over and garnish with lemon slices. Yield: 6 servings.

Lemon Butter

¼ pound (½ cup) butter
2 garlic cloves, crushed
juice of 1 lemon

1 teaspoon lemon-pepper
 seasoning

Melt butter in a small saucepan. Add garlic and cook for 2 to 3 minutes. Stir in lemon juice and seasoning. Yield: ½ cup.

Note: Pounding or flattening meat or poultry between sheets of waxed paper breaks the fibers of the meat and renders it exceptionally tender. The waxed paper gives a smooth finish to the slices.

STUFFED VEAL ROAST

4 pounds rolled veal roast
★ 1 pound bulk sausage meat
1 onion, chopped
2 garlic cloves, crushed
1 package (10 oz.) frozen chopped spinach, thawed
1 teaspoon salt

freshly ground pepper
2 tablespoons oil
1 onion, chopped
1 carrot, chopped
bouquet garni (see Note, p. 69)
1 cup chicken broth
1 cup white wine

Untie veal roast and lay out flat. Cover with a piece of waxed paper and pound with a wooden mallet or rolling pin to flatten slightly. Crumble sausage meat into a large skillet and sauté, mashing with a fork until meat begins to release its oil. Add onion and cook until limp. Add garlic and cook for 2 minutes. Squeeze as much water from spinach as possible. Add to sausage. Add salt and pepper to taste and toss well to mix. Pat the sausage-spinach mixture over the surface of the meat. Carefully re-roll, enclosing stuffing. Tie well with string. Heat oil in a large heavy-bottomed Dutch oven. Brown roast all over. Remove from pan. Add onion and carrot to pan and cook, stirring, until onion becomes limp. Return meat to Dutch oven; add *bouquet garni,* broth and wine. Bring to a boil on top of stove. Cover. Place in a preheated 350° F. oven and braise for 2½ hours. Remove meat from pan. Force liquids through a food mill or purée in a blender. Reduce over high heat to 1 cup. Slice meat, discarding strings. Place on a heated platter. Pour sauce over all and serve. Yield: 8 servings.

COUPONS FOR CONDIMENTS

Ketchup, gravy colorants, spices, herbs, mustards, chutneys, mayonnaise, garnishes, vinegars, etc.

Large firms, like General Foods, Kraft and the R.T. French Company, often publish coupons toward the purchase of condiments such as prepared mustards, Worcestershire sauce, horseradish, ketchups, etc. Mayonnaise coupons are offered regularly; pickles, relishes, herbs and spices occasionally. In compiling recipes for this chapter, I have chosen those that depend on a given condiment as the most outstanding ingredient. If the inclusion of mayonnaise, for instance, provided the unusual taste required in a certain recipe, I used it. There are recipes here for appetizers, main-course and casserole dishes and dressings. Some recipes are sophisticated and others strictly family or everyday fare. All are tried and true. I hope you enjoy them and use them every time an appropriate coupon appears.

APPETIZERS AND ONE DIP

FONDUE BOURGUIGNONNE

As I have mentioned earlier, I have always found a fondue to be a wonderful ice breaker. Reserved guests soon lose their timidity when involved with fondue fun. The sauce recipes follow the main procedure.

4 pounds beef filet or tenderloin	★ Tartar sauce
peanut oil	★ Curry sauce
★ Horseradish sauce	Anchovy butter

Partially freeze the beef filet (see Note) then cut it into cubes 1 inch thick. Fill a metal fondue dish with peanut oil, heated to 350° F. on a frying thermometer. Place over a burner in the center of a coffee table with a heatproof surface. Arrange meat cubes in an attractive serving bowl adjacent to fondue pot. Provide as many fondue forks as you have guests. Arrange 4 sauces on a tray on the coffee table. Guests spear meat, dip into boiling oil to cook, then into sauce of their choice. Have many napkins handy to protect clothing and furniture. This is a messy business. Yield: 8 servings.

Note: Partially freezing meat makes it firm, so it is much easier to cut into cubes. Be sure meat is at room temperature before dipping in hot oil.

Horseradish Sauce

1 cup commercial sour cream	2 tablespoons lemon juice
¼ cup chopped pimiento	1 teaspoon sugar
★ 2 tablespoons prepared horseradish	★ dash of Tabasco

Mix all ingredients well and pour into a serving bowl. Yield: 1½ cups.

Tartar Sauce

★ ½ cup mayonnaise	1 tablespoon snipped chives,
½ cup commercial sour cream	fresh or frozen
★ 2 teaspoons sweet pickle relish	1 teaspoon lemon juice
	1 garlic clove, crushed

Mix all ingredients well and pour into a serving bowl. Yield: 1¼ cups.

Curry Sauce

1 cup commerical sour cream
★ ½ cup mayonnaise
1 tablespoon chopped fresh
  parsley
★ 2 teaspoons curry powder

1 teaspoon lemon juice
★ 1 teaspoon Worcestershire
  sauce
¼ teaspoon salt
freshly ground pepper

Mix all ingredients well and add pepper to taste. Pour into a serving bowl. Yield: 1¾ cups.

Anchovy Butter

2 ounces (4 tablespoons)
  butter
1 can (2 oz.) anchovies
★ ½ teaspoon paprika

1 teaspoon lemon juice
★ ½ teaspoon lemon-pepper
  seasoning

Heat butter to boiling. Add drained anchovies and heat until anchovies dissolve in hot butter. Beat in remaining ingredients. Pour into serving bowl and serve warm. Yield: approximately ¾ cup.

HENNY'S MAYONNAISE CANAPÉ

One of my dearest friends claims this to be her easiest and best canapé.

★ ½ cup mayonnaise
½ cup grated Parmesan
  cheese

1 small onion, grated
1 small package (8 oz.) party
  rye rounds

Mix mayonnaise, cheese and onion. Spread generously on the rye rounds. Bake in a preheated 350° F. oven until hot and bubbly. Yield: 8 to 10 servings.

HENNY'S SARDINE CANAPÉ

Another canapé goodie from my friend.

1 can (4 oz.) sardines	½ pound American cheese
1 small package (8 oz.) party	slices
rye rounds	★ ¼ cup ketchup
	★ ¼ cup prepared Dijon mustard

Mash sardines. Spread on rye rounds. Top each with a small piece of American cheese. Mix ketchup and mustard together. Spread over cheese. Place under broiler for 2 to 3 minutes, or until cheese melts. Serve piping hot. Yield: 8 to 10 servings.

PORK-SPINACH PÂTÉ

Serve this pâté in the terrine you cooked it in.

2 packages (10 oz. each) frozen chopped spinach, thawed and drained	★ ⅛ teaspoon each of ground mace, allspice and cloves
1 pound lean boneless pork, minced	1 garlic clove, crushed
freshly ground pepper	2 tablespoons chopped fresh parsley
1 teaspoon salt	★ ¼ teaspoon dried rosemary
	★ ¼ teaspoon dried thyme
	1 egg

Combine spinach and pork. Mix in all remaining ingredients. Place in a terrine or heavy-bottomed 1½-quart baking dish with a cover. Cover first with buttered brown paper, then put dish cover on tightly. Place in a preheated 325° F. oven and bake for 1 hour. Chill. Serve in the terrine with small rounds of rye or crackers. Yield: 14 to 16 servings.

STEAK TARTARE

Some people like to eat this as a main course. I like it as an appetizer.

1½ pounds very lean, very
fresh, chopped beef sirloin
or tenderloin
½ teaspoon salt
6 anchovy filets, chopped
★ 1 tablespoon prepared Dijon
mustard

freshly ground pepper
★ dash of Tabasco
★ 1 tablespoon capers, chopped
2 egg yolks
chopped fresh parsley

Mix all ingredients except parsley very well. Mound on a serving plate and sprinkle with parsley. Serve with crackers. Yield: 10 to 12 servings.

VEGETABLE DIP

This is a great appetizer to serve to all your dieting friends.

1 small red cabbage
½ cauliflower
2 carrots
1 green pepper
3 celery ribs
½ pound whole green beans
★ ½ cup mayonnaise

★ ½ cup prepared mustard
juice of ½ lemon
★ pinch of dry mustard
★ ½ teaspoon paprika
★ ½ teaspoon garlic powder
★ ½ teaspoon onion powder

Trim cabbage. Cut top third off and cut into tiny chunks. Set aside. With a sharp knife and a spoon scoop out insides of cabbage, leaving a hollow shell about ½ inch thick. Use scooped-out portion for another meal. Cut cauliflower into bite-size flowerets. Scrape carrots and cut into julienne strips (see Note). Cut green pepper and celery into julienne strips. Trim beans and leave whole. Place tiny chunks of cabbage, cauliflowerets, carrots, green pepper, celery and beans in a deep bowl. Pour boiling water over vegetables. Allow to soak for 3 minutes, drain, dry and chill. Mix all remaining ingredients together and beat well. Pour into cabbage shell. Arrange cabbage on a large serving plate. Surround with chilled vegetables. Serve on the coffee table with cocktails. Yield: 12 servings.

Note: To cut into julienne strips means to cut into even ¼-inch strips about 2 inches long.

MAIN-COURSE AND CASSEROLE DISHES

BARBECUED CHICKEN

This chicken was always my boys' favorite meal when they were little. They still like it. The sauce is also good on spareribs.

1 frying chicken, 3½ pounds	2 tablespoons sugar
2 tablespoons oil	2 tablespoons vinegar
★ ½ cup ketchup	dash of Tabasco
★ 3 tablespoons Worcestershire sauce	

Cut broiler into serving portions. Heat oil in a skillet. Brown chicken on all sides. Drain on paper toweling. Mix remaining ingredients well. Pour a small portion into the bottom of a shallow baking pan that will accommodate chicken pieces without overlapping. Arrange chicken in a single layer on top of sauce. Pour remaining sauce over chicken. Bake in a preheated 350° F. oven for 1 hour. Yield: 4 servings.

CHARLOTTE'S HEAVENLY HASH

Here we have another wonderful dish for children. One of my friends tells me her kids would have eaten this every day, gladly.

½ pound ground beef
1 onion, chopped
1 garlic clove, crushed
4 frankfurters, cut into 1-inch
   sections

1 can (11½ oz.) bean and
   bacon soup, undiluted
1 can (1 lb.) baked beans
★ ½ cup ketchup

Sauté beef in a skillet until no longer pink. Remove beef with a slotted spoon and drain on paper toweling. Add onion to beef fat remaining in skillet. Sauté until limp. Add garlic and sauté for 2 minutes more. Pour off excess grease. Combine all remaining ingredients with meat and vegetables and return to pan. Cook over low heat, stirring occasionally, for 15 minutes. Yield: 6 servings.

LAMB KORMA

Kormas and curries are similar. For this dish, rather than buying an already prepared curry powder, you use a combination of various spices as an Indian cook would do. Curry powder is nothing more than these same combinations of spices ground together and sold as a package.

3 pounds trimmed lamb,
   cubed
2 cups plain yogurt
½ teaspoon salt
★ 1 teaspoon ground cuminseed
★ 1 teaspoon ground turmeric
★ ⅓ teaspoon ground cardamon
   peanut oil
1 onion, chopped
1 garlic clove, crushed

★ 1 teaspoon dry mustard
★ 1 teaspoon ground ginger
★ ¼ teaspoon ground cinnamon
   freshly ground pepper
★ dash of cayenne pepper
★ pinch of ground cloves
3 tablespoons flour
2 cups boiling beef broth
1 tablespoon lemon juice

Mix lamb cubes with next 5 ingredients. Toss well to incorporate. Allow to marinate overnight. The curds of the yogurt will cling to the meat and the whey (or liquid) can be lightly patted away with paper toweling just before browning. Heat oil in a large skillet. Brown meat in several stages until all is browned. Drain on paper toweling and set aside. Add onion to skillet and sauté until limp. Add garlic and next 6 ingredients and cook, stirring, for 2 to 3 minutes. Sprinkle with flour and cook, stirring, for 5 minutes longer. Off the heat, add boiling broth all at once, beating vigorously with a wire whisk to prevent lumping. Add meat to this sauce and cook over very low heat for 1 hour. Stir in lemon juice. Serve over plain boiled rice with Apple Chutney (see p. 146). Yield: 8 servings.

Microwave Cooking: Marinate meat overnight as indicated above. Microwave on "high" setting for 2 to 3 minutes. Turn meat and microwave for another 2 to 3 minutes. Sauté onion and garlic in 1 tablespoon oil until onion is limp. Scrape into meat. Mix mustard, ginger, cinnamon, pepper, cayenne, cloves and broth. Pour over meat. Microwave on "medium" setting, covered, for 30 minutes, or until meat is tender. Mix flour into ½ cup cold broth. Stir into meat. Cook on "low" setting for 4 minutes, or until gravy is thickened to your taste. Stir twice during this cooking process.

LEFTOVER BEEF WITH MUSTARD

This is a great way to use leftover, very rare, very tender beef.

4 slices of rare cooked roast beef, ½ inch thick
★ prepared Dijon mustard
fine dry bread crumbs

2 tablespoons chopped fresh parsley
oil
★ prepared horseradish

Spread each slice of beef with mustard on both sides. Mix crumbs with parsley. Roll beef in crumb mixture. Heat oil to sizzling hot in a large skillet. Quickly sauté beef slices on both sides in oil. Serve with horseradish as a garnish. Yield: 4 servings.

SCANDINAVIAN POT ROAST

The addition of caraway seeds gives this pot roast an interesting new flavor.

1 large onion, diced
1 tablespoon oil
4 pounds beef chuck or rump
   roast
salt and freshly ground pepper
¾ cup red wine

2 cups beef broth, canned or
   instant
★ 2 tablespoons caraway seeds
3 tablespoons flour
½ cup commercial sour cream

Sauté onion in oil in a heavy-bottomed stove-to-oven casserole. Brown roast on all sides in the same casserole. Season to taste. Add wine, broth and caraway seeds. Bring to a boil on top of the stove. Cover tightly and place in a preheated 350° F. oven. Braise for 2½ hours, or until meat is tender. Remove meat and set aside.

Degrease pan liquids. Beat flour into sour cream. Beat sour cream into hot pan liquids. Cook, stirring, for 10 minutes. Slice meat and arrange on a heated platter. Pour sauce over and serve. Yield: 8 servings.

SALMON WITH EGG AND CAPER SAUCE

As a Canadian, I was reared on marvelous poached Gaspé salmon; this was the most popular way to serve it. The addition of capers gives it more of a zip.

2 pounds fresh salmon in 1
   chunk (see Note)
salt and pepper

1 tablespoon butter
Egg and Caper Sauce (recipe
   follows)

Wipe salmon with a damp cloth. Salt and pepper liberally. Place on a greased rack in a deep baking dish, fitted with a lid. Dot with 1 tablespoon butter. Cover tightly. Place in a preheated 400° F. oven for 40 minutes. Meanwhile make the sauce. Serve with a generous serving of sauce. Yield: 6 servings.

Egg and Caper Sauce

2 ounces (4 tablespoons)
  butter or margarine
4 tablespoons flour
2 cups milk, scalded
1 teaspoon salt

★ ¼ teaspoon ground white
  pepper
2 eggs, hard cooked and
  sliced
★ 1 tablespoon capers, chopped

Heat butter or margarine in a saucepan. Add flour and cook, stirring, for 3 to 4 minutes. Off the heat, pour in scalded milk all at once, beating vigorously with a wire whisk. Return saucepan to heat. Add salt, pepper, eggs and capers. Cook for 5 minutes, stirring. Serve with salmon. Yield: 2½ cups.

Note: When buying a large chunk of salmon, ask for the tail. There is more meat, less bone, and the fishmonger will give you a better price.

Microwave Cooking: Place salmon in a glass or ceramic dish. Season to taste, then dot with butter. Cover with waxed paper and microwave on "high" setting for 25 minutes, or until salmon "flakes" when pricked with a fork.

To make sauce: Place butter in a small bowl. Microwave on "low" setting for 1 to 2 minutes. Add flour, milk, salt and pepper. Beat to incorporate. Microwave for 6 to 8 minutes, stirring every 2 minutes. Add eggs and capers. Heat for 30 seconds. Serve over salmon.

QUICK AND EASY SHRIMP CURRY

1 ounce (2 tablespoons) butter
2 onions, chopped
3 garlic cloves, crushed
★ 2 teaspoons curry powder
1 can (10¾ oz.) cream of
    mushroom soup

2 tablespoons commerical
    sour cream
2 pounds raw shrimps, cleaned
    and deveined
3 cups cooked rice

Heat butter in a large skillet. Add onions and sauté until limp. Add garlic and curry powder. Cook, stirring, for 2 to 3 minutes. Add undiluted soup and sour cream. Heat. Add shrimps and cook until shrimps just turn pink. Serve over plain rice. Yield: 4 to 6 servings.

SEAFOOD BAKE

This recipe is particularly good made with crab meat.

1 medium-size onion, chopped
2 ounces (4 tablespoons)
    butter, melted
¼ cup green pepper, chopped
1 cup celery, chopped
2 cups cooked seafood
    (lobster, crab, oysters or
    shrimps)

salt and freshly ground pepper
★ 1 teaspoon Worcestershire
    sauce
★ 1 cup mayonnaise
1 cup dry bread crumbs
2 tablespoons grated
    Parmesan cheese

Sauté onion in 1 ounce (2 tablespoons) of butter until limp. Mix green pepper, celery, seafood, salt and pepper to taste, Worcestershire sauce and sautéed onion. Toss well. Stir in mayonnaise and mix well to blend. Turn into 8 large individual scallop shells, ramekins, custard cups or soufflé dishes. Mix crumbs with remaining melted butter and the cheese. Sprinkle on top of seafood. Bake in a preheated 350° F. oven for 30 minutes. Yield: 4 servings.

SCALLOPED OYSTERS

This is a dish of the northern West Coast, where oysters are plentiful. Oysters are easily obtained, in season, throughout coastal United States. They are expensive but well worth the cost in my estimation.

1½ cups crushed cracker
   crumbs
½ teaspoon salt
freshly ground pepper
2 ounces (4 tablespoons)
   melted butter or margarine

1 pint shucked oysters
1 cup reconstituted nonfat dry
   milk
★ 1 teaspoon Worcestershire
   sauce

Mix cracker crumbs, salt, pepper to taste and melted butter or margarine. Toss well to mix. Place half of the oysters in a greased 2-quart casserole. Sprinkle with half of the crumb mixture. Repeat. Mix milk and Worcestershire sauce. Pour over oysters and crumbs. Bake in a preheated 350° F. oven for 30 to 40 minutes. Yield: 6 servings.

DRESSINGS

EGG AND CAPER DRESSING

This salad dressing will keep, refrigerated, for about 1 week.

1 cup salad oil
juice of 2 lemons
1 garlic clove, crushed
★ 2 tablespoon capers, chopped

1 teaspoon salt
freshly ground pepper
1 hard-cooked egg, finely
   chopped

Place all ingredients in a screw-top jar and shake vigorously before serving. Yield: 1½ cups.

ROQUEFORT DRESSING

This dressing will keep, refrigerated, for 2 weeks. Stir well before serving. If it is too thick, beat in a little oil.

1 cup commercial sour cream
★ ½ cup mayonnaise
¼ cup vinegar
★ 1 teaspoon prepared
   horseradish
★ ½ teaspoon celery salt
freshly ground pepper

1 teaspoon salt
¼ pound Roquefort cheese,
   crumbled
juice of 1 lemon
★ 1 teaspoon garlic powder
¼ cup chopped fresh parsley

Place all ingredients in a small bowl and beat vigorously to mix well. Yield: approximately 2 cups.

WINE, HERB AND BLUE-CHEESE DRESSING

This dressing will keep, refrigerated, for a long time.

2 cups salad oil
★ ½ cup vinegar
⅓ cup white wine
★ ½ teaspoon crumbled dried
   basil
★ ½ teaspoon dry mustard
★ ½ teaspoon crumbled dried
   orégano

★ ⅓ teaspoon crumbled dried
   tarragon
2 garlic cloves, crushed
2 teaspoons salt
freshly ground pepper
¼ cup chopped fresh parsley
¼ pound blue cheese,
   crumbled

Place all ingredients in a screw-top jar and shake vigorously to mix. Allow to steep for 12 hours before using. Yield: approximately 1 quart.

COUPONS FOR BAKING INGREDIENTS

There can often be savings of as much as fifty cents on such products as flour; chocolate baking items (including morsels and unsweetened chocolate); puff pastry; regular pastry; cookies; cake
mixes; pie fillings and biscuit preparations and bread doughs. The
recipes in this chapter include Main-Course Goodies; Pies, Cakes,
Tortes and Cookies and Puddings. (Chapter 11 contains the recipes
for pancakes and breads; therefore biscuit preparations or already
baked and frozen pastry shells are considered in this chapter only
where they are used as a vehicle in further preparations, for example, Seafood in Pastry Shells.)

You can save even more money if you take advantage of the
many premiums offered in and on the package of most products. I
have seen offers of $1.00 refunds on many commercial packages,
well worth the fifteen-cent stamp you use.

MAIN-COURSE GOODIES

Pastry always adds a touch of elegance to even the simplest ingredients. The recipes here all use some form of pastry.

Certainly the advent of packaged pastry mixes is a great boon to
the aspiring cook. Pastry making is one of the hardest things to
conquer in the field of cookery. The heat of your hand, when making pastry, is one thing that can ruin the final product. The more you
work it and the more water you use, the worse it is. I know; it took

me years to lick all these wretched problems. Now we have it pre-packaged and we have the food processor. The machine makes perfect pastry, absolutely foolproof. If you have a food processor, here is your recipe.

BAKED STUFFED WHOLE FISH EN CROÛTE

When you want to impress and don't have much money, try this dish. It is most elegant and you can use any whole fish, boned. Have your fishmonger remove the head, tail and bones. Bluefish, sea bass, red snapper or sea trout can be used.

2 pounds whole fish, boned, minus head and tail	1 teaspoon dried basil
	3 eggs, beaten
1 ounce (2 tablespoons) margarine or butter	salt and pepper
	★ pastry for 1-crust pie
2 scallions, greens and all, chopped	1 egg yolk mixed with 1 tablespoon water

Lay the boned fish opened flat on a board. Heat butter or margarine in a skillet. Add scallions and basil. Cook, stirring, for 2 to 3 seconds. Add beaten eggs and quickly stir with a fork for several seconds. Allow to set after this initial scrambling (see Note). Add salt and pepper to taste to the eggs. Roll the "omelet" into the same shape as the fish and lay on the lower half of fish. Fold the top half over, enclosing omelet. Roll out pastry. Lay omelet stuffed fish in the middle. Fold dough around fish, securing edges well. Carefully transfer to a shallow baking dish. Brush all over with egg wash. Bake in a preheated 400° F. oven for 35 minutes. Remove from oven and transfer to a heated platter. Allow to sit for 10 to 15 minutes before slicing. Cut into 1½ inch slices. Serve with a simple tossed salad, dressed à la vinaigrette (see Comment). Yield: 4 to 6 servings.

Note: Treat the egg batter as you would scrambled eggs: quickly stir for several seconds as soon as eggs are added to the skillet, to ensure a lighter, puffier "omelet." It only takes a few quick stirs with a fork. Then allow the eggs to set as you would an ordinary omelet. Once set, fold one half over the other and turn out onto a platter.

Comment: À *la* vinaigrette usually means a dressing made with 1 part oil, ¼ to ⅓ part vinegar, salt, pepper and a dash of dry mustard.

HANDMADE PASTRY

If you do not have a food processor and would like to try making your own pastry, follow this recipe, trying to work the dough as little as possible. Try cutting in the shortening with 2 knives or a pastry blender, rather than using your hands. When adding the shortening, add half, cut in, then add the other half. Stir in half of the water, then the other half. Keep stirring until pastry begins to lump and forms a ball.

★ 2 cups all-purpose flour
   dash of salt
★ 7 ounces (⅞ cup) cold margarine, or shortening
   6 tablespoons ice water

Place flour in a bowl. Add salt. Cut in margarine or shortening until crumbly. Add ice water and stir until thoroughly incorporated. Yield: pastry for one 2-crust pie or two 1-crust pies.

Comment: Many times I suggest the use of equipment in the kitchen that young people just starting out may not have and cannot afford. Food processors are expensive and may be considered a luxury; blenders somewhat less so. A food mill does essentially the same thing. It is an old-fashioned device still sold in all department stores and in hardware stores. It is quite inexpensive, easy to operate and simple to clean. While it does not do as many things the other devices do, it is excellent for puréeing, and better than a blender or a food processsor for removing seeds and fibers.

An electric mixer is invaluable in the kitchen. If you do not have one, a portable hand mixer works quite well. Failing that, an egg beater will do for some things, like beating egg whites. A purist would beat egg whites or heavy cream in an unlined copper bowl with a large balloon whisk. The acid in the copper helps the egg whites to mount, resulting in an airier, lighter confection.

CHICKEN POT PIE

1 onion, chopped
3 ounces (6 tablespoons)
   margarine or butter
1 garlic clove, crushed
1 teaspoon dried basil
★ 4 tablespoons flour
1½ cups boiling chicken broth,
   canned, instant or fresh
½ cup light cream, scalded
1 teaspoon salt
freshly ground pepper
½ cup grated Cheddar or
   Parmesan cheese

¼ pound sliced mushrooms
1 cup cooked carrot rings
1 package (10 oz.) frozen
   peas, cooked
2 cups chunks of cooked
   chicken
¼ cup chopped fresh parsley
★ pastry for 1-crust pie
   or
1 roll of (7½ oz. package)
   refrigerated biscuits
1 egg yolk mixed with 1
   tablespoon water (see Note)

Sauté onion in 2 ounces (4 tablespoons) butter or margarine until limp. Add garlic and basil. Cook for 1 to 2 minutes. Sprinkle with flour and cook, stirring, for 2 to 3 minutes. Off the heat, add boiling broth all at once (see Comment, p. 92), beating vigorously with a wire whisk. Stir in cream, salt, pepper to taste and cheese. Return to heat and cook, stirring, until cheese melts. Sauté mushrooms in remaining butter in a separate small pan. Add mushrooms, vegetables (see Comment), chicken and parsley to the sauce. Turn into a 2-quart casserole. Roll out the pastry and drape it over top of casserole. Trim and crimp edges. Brush with egg wash. If using biscuit dough, place uncooked biscuits on top of pie, barely touching each other. Brush with egg wash. Bake in a preheated 425° F. oven for 15 minutes. Reduce heat to 350° F. and bake for another 25 minutes. Yield: 6 to 8 servings.

Note: An egg yolk beaten with water is called an egg wash. It is used to give a shiny dark brown glaze to breads and pastries.

Comment: If you have a coupon for frozen vegetables in cheese sauce, use them for this recipe. Eliminate the grated cheese from the sauce. You might add any vegetable you wish; my ingredients are suggestions. Anything complements chicken.

Microwave Cooking: Bake in a plastic, ceramic or glass dish on "high" setting for 13 to 15 minutes. Add pastry or biscuits and bake on "medium" setting for 6 to 8 minutes. Rotate dish every 3 minutes.

ITALIAN POTATO PIE

When I was a chef, this was easily the most successful potato dish I served. The best part about it was that it improved with age. I could bake it ahead and put it on the back of the stove to keep warm. Or it could be frozen and reheated after the initial baking. It tasted just as good the second day as the first. It could be served as a starch at dinner, or as the main luncheon dish with a tossed salad.

4 or 5 large Idaho potatos	1 cup chopped fresh parsley
★ pastry for 2-crust 9-inch pie	½ cup heavy cream
2 garlic cloves, crushed	1 egg yolk mixed with 1
salt and pepper	tablespoon water

Peel potatoes and slice very thin. Place in a basin of cold water to prevent discoloration. Roll out half of the pastry; use to line a 9-inch deep pie plate. Arrange one quarter of the potato slices, well drained and dried on paper toweling, in the bottom of the pastry. Sprinkle with one quarter of the garlic, salt and pepper to taste and ¼ cup parsley. Repeat until all potatoes, seasoning and parsley are used (3 more layers). Roll out remaining pastry and drape over top. Crimp edges attractively. Make a slash in the center. Carefully pour cream through this hole. Brush pastry with egg wash. Bake in a preheated 425° F. oven for 1 hour. Allow to sit for 10 to 15 minutes before slicing (see Comment). Yield: 8 to 10 servings.

Comment: Most pies, pastries and tortes, like roasts, are easier to cut and serve if they are allowed to rest before being sliced. Pastries, pies and tortes settle somewhat, resulting in a firmer body.

Microwave Cooking: Reheat at "medium-high" setting for 5 to 7 minutes per slice.

SEAFOOD IN PASTRY SHELLS

Once in a while you may be lucky enough to find some seafood on sale, or your local grocer may give you a coupon applied to shrimps or scallops, or even crab meat. But lobster? NEVER!! This is a really show-offy sort of dish; keep it for the boss or your most difficult in-laws.

1 onion, chopped
3 ounces (6 tablespoons) butter or margarine
1 garlic clove, crushed
★ 4 tablespoons flour
1½ cups bottled clam juice, boiling
½ teaspoon salt
freshly ground pepper
½ cup heavy cream, scalded (see Note)

¼ pound mushrooms, sliced
2 ounces sherry
1½ pounds cooked shrimps, scallops, crab meat or lobster
★ 6 pastry shells made from puff paste or regular pastry, or purchased already made
½ cup chopped fresh parsley

Sauté onion in 2 ounces (4 tablespoons) butter or margarine until limp. Add garlic and sauté for another 1 minute. Sprinkle with flour and cook, stirring, for 2 to 3 minutes. Take off heat and add all the boiling clam juice at once. Beat vigorously with a wire whisk (see Comment). Add salt, pepper to taste and cream. Return to heat and cook for 2 to 3 minutes. Sauté mushrooms in remaining butter in a separate small pan. Stir mushrooms, sherry and seafood into the sauce. Heat pastry shells in a preheated 350° F. oven for 5 minutes. Fill with seafood; sprinkle with parsley. Serve without delay. Yield: 6 servings.

Note: Always scald milk products before adding them to a hot sauce. This prevents curdling. To scald, bring to just under the boil. Bubbles will appear around edges of milk and a film will form on top.

Comment: A rule of thumb in making sauces: 1 tablespoon fat + 1 tablespoon flour + 1 cup liquid will make a thin sauce; 2 tablespoons fat + 2 tablespoons flour + 1 cup of liquid will make a medium thick sauce; 3 tablespoons fat + 3 tablespoons flour + 1 cup liquid makes a thick sauce. When making sauces always take the *roux* off the heat before adding the liquid. Beat the boiling liquid in very hard with a wire whisk, pouring it onto the *roux* all at once. This prevents lumping.

Microwave Cooking: Fill cold shells with seafood ahead of time. Heat filled shells on "high" setting for 4 minutes.

FOOD PROCESSOR PÂTE BRISÉE (Plain Pastry)

Use one of those margarine coupons you have tucked away and double the following recipe. Divide it into 4 parts and freeze what you don't use.

★ 2 cups all-purpose flour ⅔ cup cold margarine, cut into
dash of salt chunks
4 to 5 tablespoons cold water

Place flour in the bowl of a food processor fitted with the steel blade. Add salt and margarine. Process until crumbly. With machine running, add water only until dough leaves the sides of the jar. Divide into halves and wrap each section in waxed paper. Refrigerate until ready to use. Yield: pastry for one 2-crust pie or two 1-crust pies.

Comment: Bulk white shortening can be substituted for margarine if so desired. I use margarine because it is easier to measure. It is also cheaper. Buy the cheapest. You do not need the best corn-oil margarines for baking. To measure bulk shortenings, pour into a cup measure (in this case) ⅓ cup water, then force in shortening until the water level reaches the full mark. Lightly salted margarines do not make a measurable difference in the final product; if salt is a problem for you, merely cut down or eliminate the salt in the recipe.

PIES, CAKES, TORTES AND COOKIES

Most of these recipes require little effort in preparation. I have used the food products for which coupons most often appear. Why not put them to good use in everyday desserts that appeal to all those sweet-toothed people wandering around America? Think of all the husbands and children this section will make happy!

CHOCOLATE PIE

When my boys were little they would eat chocolate pie until it oozed from their ears. In self-defense I started using commercial pudding mixes. By necessity they had to be those that were cooked, not the instant variety. The recipe following was my compromise.

1 Cereal Crumb Crust (p. 38)
      or
2 cups cookie or cracker
    crumbs
1 tablespoon granulated sugar
2⅔ ounces (⅓ cup) melted
    butter or margarine

★ 2 packages (4 oz. each)
    chocolate pudding and pie
    filling
3 ounces semisweet chocolate,
    grated
1 cup heavy cream
2 tablespoons confectioners'
    sugar

Use cereal pie crust or make a crumb crust by mixing crumbs with granulated sugar and margarine. Pat into a deep 9-inch pie plate. Bake in a preheated 325° F. oven for 10 minutes. Cool. Prepare pudding according to package directions (see Note). When it has cooled, fold in all but 3 tablespoons of the grated chocolate. Pour into the prepared pie shell. Whip the cream and sweeten with confectioners' sugar. Top pie with cream and sprinkle with remaining grated chocolate. Chill well before serving. Yield: 8 to 10 servings.

Note: When making pie or pudding fillings, place a sheet of waxed paper or clear plastic over the top of the container while it is cooling. This prevents formation of a skin on top.

LEMON TORTE

A true torte is an airy dessert, lighter than a cake as we know it, made with ground nuts and beaten egg whites and little, if any, flour. The torte was a specialty of Austria and Hungary. While this is not a true torte, it resembles it in having many layers and in being decorated with whipped cream rather than a conventional icing or frosting.

★ 1 box (18½ oz.) cake mix (yellow, white, orange or lemon)
Lemon Curd (recipe follows)
2 cups heavy cream

★ 4 tablespoons confectioners' sugar
1 teaspoon vanilla extract
shaved almonds

Bake the cake in 2 pans, according to package instructions. Cool on a rack. Make lemon curd. Cut cake layers horizontally into halves (see Note). Place 1 layer on a serving plate. Spread with one third of the lemon curd. Repeat with layer of cake and curd, twice. Place fourth cake layer on top. Whip cream with confectioners' sugar until stiff. Fold in vanilla. Ice the torte with whipped cream. Garnish with shaved almonds. Chill thoroughly before serving. Yield: 10 to 12 servings.

Lemon Curd

4 egg yolks
½ cup sugar
dash of salt

¼ cup lemon juice
grated rind of 1 lemon
½ cup heavy cream, whipped

Mix egg yolks, sugar, salt, lemon juice and grated rind in the top part of a double boiler. Stir over hot water until mixture is thick and smooth. Remove from heat and cool. Fold in heavy cream.

Note: When slicing a cake layer into halves, mark one edge with a slash before cutting. When reassembling cake, match up slashes to be sure the layers are even.

WHIPPED CREAM TOPPING

1 cup heavy cream
★ 2 tablespoons confectioners' sugar
1 teaspoon vanilla extract

Beat cream until soft peaks form. Beat in sugar and vanilla. Spread over entire surface of cake. Sprinkle top with cake crumbs or shaved chocolate.

Comment: We have a food processor mania in this country. All you folk who resist this pressure and do not have a food processor don't know what you are missing. It is the finest thing to hit the food industry since fire. If you still resist my sales pitch, this is the way to make frostings by hand: First cream the soft margarine or cream cheese until fluffy. Gradually beat in sugar until crumbly. Gradually add heavy cream until mixture is of spreading consistency. If you have a mixer, then do the whole process electrically.

ANGEL SURPRISE CAKE

This is truly a surprise cake. When you cut into it, you find a delicious creamy filling. You can substitute an angel-food cake mix if you don't want to make the cake from scratch.

★ 1¼ cups cake flour
★ 1¾ cups sugar
1¾ cups egg whites, at room temperature
½ teaspoon salt
1½ teaspoons cream of tartar

2 teaspoons vanilla extract
½ teaspoon almond extract
Lemon Filling (recipe follows)
2 cups heavy cream
4 tablespoons confectioners' sugar

Sift flour and ¾ cup sugar three times. Beat egg whites until soft peaks form. Beat in salt and cream of tartar. Gradually beat in remaining 1 cup sugar. Beat until meringue is very stiff. Fold one quarter of the flour mixture into the meringue. Fold in remaining dry ingredients carefully, along with 1 teaspoon vanilla and the almond extract. Turn into an *ungreased* 10-inch angel-food tube pan. Bake in a preheated 375° F. oven for 35 to 40 minutes. Invert the cake still in the pan (see Note) and allow to cool completely, standing on little legs attached to tube pan. If cake is too high to stand on little legs, invert the tube pan on a wine bottle or a funnel inserted through the hole of the tube. While cake is cooling, prepare lemon filling. When cool, set pan upright and remove the cake.

Cut one quarter of the cake off the top. Using a sharp knife cut out the inside of lower portion of cake, leaving a ½-inch shell with a cavity in the middle. (Use insides for English Trifle, p. 110.) Fill cavity with lemon filling. Replace top quarter of cake. Whip the cream and sweeten with the confectioners' sugar. Add remaining 1 teaspoon vanilla. Frost cake with sweetened whipped cream. Chill thoroughly before serving. Yield: 10 to 12 servings.

Lemon Filling

4 egg yolks	½ cup lemon juice
⅔ cup sugar	grated rind of 1 lemon
★ 2 tablespoons cornstarch	1 tablespoon butter or
1 cup water	margarine

Place egg yolks, sugar, cornstarch and water in the top part of a double boiler. Beat well with a wire whisk. Cook over boiling water, stirring, until thick and smooth, approximately 10 minutes. Remove from heat and stir in lemon juice, grated rind and butter or margarine. Cover with waxed paper and cool. Use to fill angel cake.

Instead of lemon filling, you might use chocolate, vanilla or butterscotch pudding and pie mix. Use 2 packages (approximately 3⅝ oz. each) and only two thirds of the milk required on the package. The remaining one third liquid should be heavy cream, whipped, and folded into the cooled pudding.

Note: Angel-food cakes are baked in ungreased pans to allow the meringuelike batter to cling to the sides of the pan, hence ensuring a higher rising of the batter. The pan is then inverted to prevent cake "settling" as it cools.

CRUMB CAKE

Here's an easy, delicious way to make use of a lot of your coupons at once. This cake uses cookie crumbs rather than flour as its starch ingredient. One might even substitute cereal crumbs if so desired.

¼ pound (½ cup) butter or margarine
★ 1 cup sugar
★ ¼ teaspoon baking powder

1½ cups vanilla or chocolate cookie crumbs (see Note)
3 eggs
1 cup chopped nuts
1⅓ cups shredded coconut

Grease, then flour a 9-inch-square pan, 2 inches deep. Cream butter or margarine and sugar well. Stir in baking powder and crumbs. Add eggs, one at a time, beating well after each addition. Fold in nuts and coconut. Pour into the prepared pan. Bake in a preheated 325° F. oven for 35 minutes. Spread with frosting of your choice (see following recipes). Yield: 8 servings.

Note: A food processor or blender is the best way to make crumbs. Place vanilla or chocolate wafers, or graham crackers, in the bowl and process until fine. If you do not have a processor or blender, place the wafers or crackers in a plastic bag and press with a rolling pin until fine.

CHOCOLATE FROSTING

★ 2 cups confectioners' sugar
2½ ounces (5 tablespoons) soft margarine

⅓ cup cocoa powder
2 tablespoons heavy cream

Place sugar in the bowl of a food processor or mixer. Add margarine and blend until crumbly. Add cocoa and blend well. Beat in cream to give spreading consistency. Yield: frosting for 2-layer cake.

CREAM-CHEESE FROSTING

3 ounces cream cheese
★ 2 cups confectioners' sugar,
   sifted

1 teaspoon vanilla extract
dash of salt
2 tablespoons heavy cream

Place cream cheese in the bowl of a food processor or mixer. Cream well. Add sugar and blend until crumbly. Add vanilla, salt and enough cream to give good spreading consistency. Yield: frosting for 2-layer cake.

CHEATING APPLE CAKE

This is really a cheat, this cake! You don't do anything but put things together. If your coupon is for cherry filling rather than apple, add ginger instead of cinnamon and proceed accordingly. It will taste just as good.

★ 2 cans (1 lb. each) apple filling
1 teaspoon ground cinnamon
½ cup chopped walnuts

★ 1 box (18½ oz.) white or
   yellow cake mix
   ice cream

Grease a baking pan 8 x 10 x 2 inches very well. Sprinkle with flour, then shake excess flour from pan. Mix apple filling with cinnamon and spread in bottom of pan. Sprinkle with walnuts. Mix cake according to package instructions. Spread over apple-nut filling. Bake in a preheated 350° F. oven for 30 minutes, or until a toothpick inserted in the middle of the cake comes out clean. Serve warm or cold with ice cream. Yield: 10 to 12 servings.

Comment: In addition to the toothpick method, there are other ways of testing cakes. When the cake shrinks from the sides of the pan and springs back when surface is pressed with a finger, it is done. When your house is permeated with that wonderful baking cake odor, it means your cake will probably be done in about 5 minutes.

NO-BAKE COOKIES ★★★★★★★★★★★★★★★★★

Our first cookies are all no-bake. Kids love to make these and they are foolproof. The mess is minimal and they require little effort. Try them at Christmastime; they make lovely house gifts and the children will feel they have truly contributed to the spirit of the occasion.

CHEWY BALLS

★ 1 package (12 oz.) chocolate, butterscotch or peanut butter morsels
1 can (14 oz.) sweetened condensed milk

2 cups crushed cereal of your choice
★ confectioners' sugar

Melt morsels in the top part of a double boiler over hot water or in a microwave oven. Add condensed milk and cereal crumbs. Drop by spoonful onto a sheet of waxed paper. Cool in the refrigerator until firm. Roll into balls, then roll in confectioners' sugar. Yield: 48 balls.

NANAIMO SQUARES

This recipe was given to me by my Canadian family. Nanaimo is a navy yard on Vancouver Island off the West Coast of Canada. How these bars acquired this name is beyond me, but they taste great.

½ pound (1 cup) plus 1 tablespoon butter
¼ cup granulated sugar
★ 1 ounce (1 square) unsweetened chocolate
1 teaspoon vanilla extract
1 egg
2 cups ground graham-cracker crumbs

½ cup chopped walnuts or pecans
1 cup moist, flaked coconut
★ 2 tablespoons instant vanilla pudding mix
3 tablespoons milk
★ 2 cups confectioners' sugar
★ 4 ounces semisweet chocolate

Place ¼ pound butter, the granulated sugar, unsweetened chocolate and vanilla in the top part of a double boiler. Cook over boiling water until chocolate melts. Add egg and beat well to mix. Cook over boiling water for 5 minutes. Remove from heat and stir in cracker crumbs, nuts and coconut. Press into the bottom of a 9-inch square pan that is 2 inches deep. Chill in refrigerator for 15 minutes.

Cream ¼ pound softened butter, the instant pudding mix and milk together. Mix in confectioners' sugar. Combine thoroughly. Spread over crumb mixture. Chill for another 15 minutes. Melt semi-sweet chocolate and 1 tablespoon butter together. Mix well. Spread over second layer. Chill until chocolate is almost hard. Score top lightly, marking off 1-inch squares. Chill until hard. Cut into squares. Yield: 81 squares. These bars are incredibly rich.

CHOCOLATE DIPS

I used to dribble cookies in this chocolate glaze by the hour when my boys were little. They suggested I roll them in ground nuts or coconut. They were certainly right; the cookies tasted even better than before. You too can do that if you wish; it makes these cookies very festive.

★ 1 cup sifted confectioners'
    sugar
¾ cup peanut butter
1 egg, slightly beaten
1 cup moist flaked coconut
1 cup finely chopped figs,
    dates or prunes
½ cup finely chopped walnuts

dash of salt
¼ teaspoon vanilla extract
★ 1 package (12 oz.) chocolate
    morsels
2 tablespoons milk
1 cup finely chopped walnuts
    or shredded coconut

Combine sugar and peanut butter in a bowl. Beat in egg. Stir in coconut, fruit, walnuts, salt and vanilla. Roll into logs or balls. Chill for several hours. Melt chocolate morsels with the milk. Dip the logs or balls into melted chocolate. Roll in nuts or coconut. Chill again. Yield: 30 cookies.

BAKED COOKIES ★★★★★★★★★★★★★★★★★

These few recipes are the best of my collection. They are all geared to Christmas.

BEST COOKIES

I have these cookies listed under "best cookies" in my professional chef file, so this gives you some idea of how popular these are.

2½ cups flour
½ teaspoon salt
10 ounces (1¼ cups)
  margarine

★ ¾ cup confectioners' sugar
1 teaspoon vanilla extract
1¼ cuts rolled oats

Sift flour and salt. Cream margarine, sugar and vanilla. Add flour mixture and rolled oats. Form into balls or logs. Bake on a greased cookie sheet in a preheated 350° F. oven for 25 minutes. Cool on a rack. Decorate (suggestions follow). Yield: 75 to 80 cookies.

Decorations

Melt 2 packages (6 oz. each) semisweet chocolate bits with ¼ cup milk. Dip rolls or balls in this chocolate mixture, then immediately roll in one of the following: chocolate sprinkles; nonpareils (colored sprinkles); coconut; chopped nuts of your choice.

GINGERBREAD MEN

What would Christmas be like without a good chewy gingerbread man for the children? This is a particularly good recipe. They keep very well, can be made ahead and frozen or stored in a cool dry place.

★ 1 cup brown sugar
★ ½ cup molasses
  ½ cup applesauce
  2 ounces (¼ cup) margarine
  1 egg
  ½ cup ground almonds

3 cups flour
¼ teaspoon ground cloves
¼ teaspoon ground ginger
¼ teaspoon baking soda
raisins

Combine first 4 ingredients in a small saucepan. Boil for 5 minutes. Cool. Add egg and almonds. Mix flour with spices and baking soda. Combine all together, then chill. Roll a ball about the size of an egg in the palms of the hands. Press onto a cookie sheet to form the body. Roll another ball the size of a quarter. Press in place for the head. Roll 4 cylinders for arms and legs. Press in place. Place raisins for eyes, nose, mouth and buttons down front. Bake in a preheated 325° F. oven for 12 minutes. Cool. Yield: 2 dozen.

PUDDINGS

GINGER PUDDING

This is a delectable ending to a winter's meal, but it will win applause at any season.

★ ¼ pound (½ cup) margarine
1 can or jar (1 lb.) applesauce
1 teaspoon ground cinnamon
★ 1 package (14 oz.)
gingerbread mix

1 cup heavy cream
★ 2 tablespoons confectioners'
sugar
1 teaspoon vanilla extract

Melt margarine and pour into a 2-quart casserole. Pour applesauce over margarine. Sprinkle with cinnamon. Mix gingerbread according to package instructions. Pour carefully over applesauce. Cover tightly. Bake in a preheated 350° F. oven for 40 minutes. Beat cream with sugar until stiff. Fold in vanilla. Serve pudding warm with whipped cream. Yield: 8 servings.

FUDGE PUDDING

1½ cups packaged biscuit mix
★ ½ cup granulated sugar
½ cup milk
½ cup brown sugar

¾ cup chopped nuts
1½ cups boiling water
★ 1 package (6 oz.) semisweet
chocolate bits

Grease a baking pan 10 x 6 x 1½ inches. Combine biscuit mix and granulated sugar. Stir in the milk. Drop batter by spoonfuls into bottom of pan, making 6 mounds. Sprinkle each mound with brown sugar and nuts. Dissolve chocolate in boiling water, stir until smooth, and pour over biscuit mounds. Bake in a preheated 350° F. oven for 35 minutes. Spoon chocolate syrup from pan over biscuits before serving. Yield: 6 servings.

COUPONS FOR COMMERCIAL CAKES, PIES AND COOKIES

This is a broad category. Not only are many coupons issued toward the purchase of these items, but stores often have specials featuring commercially prepared baked products. Day-old cakes are offered at greatly reduced rates, and while they are often not the best of their kind, they can be incorporated in many excellent desserts.

Little can be done with commercially produced pies, other than serving them garnished with ice cream or a whipped topping. Brushing a 2-crust pie with an egg wash (see Note, p. 90), then sprinkling with granulated sugar before baking can bring up the taste. A 1-crust pie may benefit from a dusting of freshly grated nutmeg or a generous sprinkling of cinnamon. Cream pies and cheesecakes improve when served with a Raspberry or Strawberry Sauce (pp. 120 and 153), or merely open a can of crushed pineapple, drain well, then mound on top of the pie, sprinkle with rum or sherry and serve.

The following recipes are presented in two groups, the first using commercial cakes, your own homemade or leftovers; the second packaged cookies, wafers and crackers.

UNBAKED DESSERTS USING CAKE BASE

Some of these desserts are very easy to prepare; they are merely a matter of assembly. Others, however, are not so easy—Baked Alaska, for instance. It sometimes frightens people, but armed with a few rules to follow, you can do it with the flourish of an expert. Most of these recipes I would consider busy-day recipes. You can fall back on them when you want to show off but don't have the time to fuss. They can also be very economical, allowing you to take advantage of the day-old table or those many coupons issued every month for commercial products that can be improved with a little home effort.

BAKED ALASKA

Be sure to start this winner at least a day ahead, as the ice cream must freeze for at least 24 hours.

★ stale cake (sponge, pound,
   white, yellow, angel-food, etc.)
★ ice cream of your choice
   4 egg whites, at room
   temperature (see Note 1)

dash of salt
1 cup sugar
1 teaspoon vanilla extract

Cut 6 squares, approximately 3 inches square and ½ inch thick, from stale cake. Place on a greased jellyroll pan. Refrigerate. Scoop 6 large balls of ice cream and place on a square of waxed paper. Freeze until very hard. This will take at least 24 hours. It is imperative that the ice cream be rock hard.

Just before serving place egg whites in the bowl of an electric mixer. Beat with salt until soft peaks form. Gradually add sugar, 1 teaspoon at a time, until all is incorporated. Beat in vanilla. Place a ball of ice cream on each square of cake. Smooth one sixth of the meringue over each serving, swirling it to form attractive peaks. Bake in a preheated 450° F. oven for no more than 5 minutes. As soon as the meringue appears to be browning, immediately remove from oven, transfer to a serving platter, and serve at once. Yield: 6 servings.

Variation: Heat ½ cup rum until hot but not boiling (see Note 2). Ignite rum with a match and pour some flaming over each serving. Bring to the table flaming.

Note 1: Egg whites will mount better and hold more air if they are at room temperature or slightly warmed before beating. If whites are beaten by hand in a copper bowl, the acid from the unlined copper helps to stabilize the foam. If you are not using a copper bowl, the addition of cream of tartar to egg whites is needed to provide acid for stabilization.

Note 2: Liquor or liqueurs must be warmed before igniting, otherwise they will not light. If boiling, they will explode and sear your hair if you are leaning too close. They should be heated to approximately 135° F. If you stick your finger in the liquor it should be hot, but not unbearable.

ICEBOX CASSATA

This is not really a *cassata,* which is an Italian dessert usually made with candied fruits and ice creams, but it's much quicker to make and always a popular dessert.

★ 1 frozen pound cake (16 oz.)
1 jar (12 oz.) chocolate fudge
   topping
½ gallon vanilla ice cream,
   softened

Chocolate Frosting (p. 98)
1 ounce German semisweet
   chocolate or semisweet
   baking chocolate

Slice the cake horizontally into 4 thin layers. Place 1 layer on a serving dish. Spread with fudge sauce. Top with a layer of softened ice cream. Repeat until all cake, sauce and ice cream are used. Ice with chocolate frosting. Place in the freezer. Remove from freezer 30 minutes before serving. Using a sharp paring knife or potato peeler, shave semisweet chocolate curls over top of cake. Yield: 8 servings.

Comment: Chocolate should always be at room temperature before shaving. If too cold, the curls will crumble as you make them.

CHARLOTTE RUSSE

When I was a child, we could purchase Charlotte Russe in little individual cups. My dad would bring them home from the local *pâtisserie* and nothing tasted better; they were our truest treat. Now I prefer a large molded Charlotte Russe that will serve at least 8 people. Brought to the table garnished with strawberries or raspberries and whipped cream, it is a real *pièce de résistance!*

8 egg yolks (see Comment)
1 cup granulated sugar
2 cups milk, scalded
2 envelopes unflavored gelatin
¼ cup water
2 ounces rum
3 cups heavy cream

★ 15 to 20 ladyfingers, split
2 tablespoons confectioners' sugar
1 teaspoon vanilla extract
1 pint strawberries or raspberries, cleaned

Beat egg yolks with granulated sugar in the top part of a double boiler. Very slowly pour scalded milk over egg mixture, beating constantly. Cook over boiling water, stirring constantly, until the custard is thick and coats the back of a metal spoon. Soften gelatin in ¼ cup water, then stir into hot custard and dissolve it. Cool. Stir in rum. Whip 2 cups heavy cream until stiff, and fold into the custard.

Place a ring of split lady fingers in the bottom of a charlotte mold or a 2-quart soufflé dish. (Cut ladyfingers into pie-shaped, very thin wedges so that they will fit together in a fan-shape to make a circle.) Stand more split ladyfingers upright around edges of dish, pressing firmly to sides to secure in place. Dampening them lightly with rum will aid in securing them, but don't overdo or they will become soggy. Fill cavity with the custard. Place in the refrigerator until firm. Unmold on a chilled platter. To unmold, slip a thin knife down the sides of the charlotte mold and carefully press lightly to release. Place an inverted platter over top of mold. Turn upside down and the charlotte should fall into place. Beat remaining 1 cup of heavy cream with confectioners' sugar until stiff. Stir in vanilla. Garnish Charlotte Russe with cream and berries. Serve at once. Yield: 8 to 10 servings.

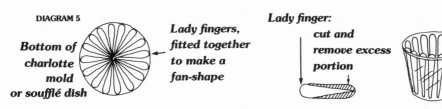

DIAGRAM 5

Bottom of charlotte mold or soufflé dish

Lady fingers, fitted together to make a fan-shape

Lady finger: cut and remove excess portion

Comment: Egg whites freeze beautifully. Whenever a recipe calls for egg yolks only, pour the separated whites into a plastic cup. If you have a favorite recipe calling for 3 egg whites, freeze the required amount. When frozen solid, turn the cup upside down under hot running water. When the solid lump is released, place in a labeled plastic bag and place in the freezer. Angel-food cakes, for instance, take 1¾ cups egg whites to do a good job (see p. 96), accumulate them in this way, for they will keep in the freezer for 4 months. Just defrost, bring to room temperature, proceed with the recipe.

BERRY OR PEACH SHORTCAKE

Correctly a shortcake is a biscuit, very buttery and rich, that is split and filled. However, I have found that people really enjoy "short-cakes" that are made from sponge and angel-food cakes. These cakes do tend to become soggy if made too far in advance. To avoid that, assemble the cake just before serving. Have the cream whipped, the fruit crushed and the cake split, then just arrange at-tractively while the coffee is perking.

★ 1 commercial angel-food
   tubular cake (14 oz.)
2 cups crushed and sweetened
   strawberries, raspberries or
   peaches

2 cups heavy cream
2 tablespoons sugar
1 teaspoon vanilla extract
1 cup whole berries or peach
   slices

Split angel-food into halves, forming 2 thick layers. Place lower half on a serving platter. Pour half of the crushed fruit over this layer. Place the second layer on top and spread with remaining fruit. Whip the cream, sweeten with sugar and flavor with vanilla. Completely frost cake with whipped cream. Garnish with whole berries or sliced peaches. Yield: 10 to 12 servings.

ENGLISH TRIFLE

Try this dessert when you find day-old cake on sale in the super-market, or use any cake that you consider slightly over the hill. My mother-in-law used to bring me a sponge cake that was so dry it was impossible to eat. I made a trifle or two with it and this became a family tradition. I used so much rum to allay the rubbery quality of the cake that my guests staggered from the table.

2 cups milk (see Note)	★ 4 cups broken pieces of stale
3 egg yolks	cake
⅓ cup sugar	4 tablespoons raspberry jam
1 teaspoon vanilla extract	4 ounces rum or sherry
	grated nutmeg

Scald milk. Beat egg yolks with sugar. Gradually beat in hot milk. Pour into the top part of a double boiler and cook over hot water, stirring, until custard coats the back of a metal spoon, about 10 minutes. Remove from heat and stir in vanilla. Cool.

Place one quarter of the cake pieces in the bottom of an elegant serving dish. Dot with 1 tablespoon jam. Sprinkle with 1 ounce of the rum or sherry. Pour one quarter of the custard over this. Repeat this process three times. Sprinkle with nutmeg. Chill before serving. Yield: 8 servings.

Note: You may use nonfat dry milk if you prefer. Reconstitute according to package instructions and proceed with recipe. To scald milk, heat to just under the boiling point. When bubbles appear around the edges and a skin forms on top, milk is scalded.

DESSERT FONDUE

This is a great dessert if you are serving just coffee and a sweet and you want to involve a group of people who do not know each other very well. All fondues are "ice-breakers." The participation is what does it.

★ 1 day-old sponge cake or angel-food cake (14 oz.)
2 cups pear juice (see Note)
juice of 1 lemon
juice of 1 lime

1 teaspoon freshly grated gingerroot
2 tablespoons cornstarch
4 ounces Marsala wine
1 tablespoon butter

Cut cake into 2-inch cubes. Arrange attractively in a basket or bowl. Place pear juice in a saucepan. Add lemon and lime juices and gingerroot. Mix cornstarch with Marsala wine. Bring juice to a boil, and stir in cornstarch mixture. Cook until clear and thickened. Stir in butter. Pour sauce into a fondue dish. Guests spear a piece of cake with a fondue fork, dip into sauce and eat. Be sure to supply lots of napkins; fondue is a messy business, but fun. Yield: 10 to 12 servings.

Variation: Cocoa Glaze (p. 157) can also be served, to provide 2 sauces, especially if you have a larger group.

Note: Juice from canned pears works admirably for this dessert. Bottled pear juice is a trifle too sweet for this purpose.

UNBAKED DESSERTS USING COOKIES, WAFERS AND CRACKERS AS A BASE

BISCUIT TORTONI

This is a typical Italian dessert. Many Italian desserts are very sweet and overly fancy, but this is relatively simple, and has the advantage of being ready in advance.

★ 1 cup stale coconut macaroon
  crumbs
1 envelope unflavored gelatin
¼ cup water
1 cup milk, scalded

2 eggs
½ cup sugar
1½ ounces dark rum
1 cup heavy cream, whipped
12 maraschino cherries

Place 12 paper cupcake liners in muffin tins. Sprinkle half of the crumbs in the bottom of the liners. Reserve remaining crumbs. Soften gelatin in water. Stir into hot milk until dissolved. Beat eggs until foamy. Gradually beat in sugar. Beat until thick and lemon-colored. Slowly stir in gelatin mixture. Add rum. Chill until syrupy. Fold in whipped cream. Pour into prepared cups. Sprinkle with remaining crumbs. Top each with a cherry. Freeze until firm. Yield: 12 servings.

FROZEN PUMPKIN PIE

Ginger and pumpkin have a natural affinity. This may be a pleasing version of the inevitable pumpkin pie at Thanksgiving. The best part is you can make it weeks ahead and have one less thing to do during that rushed season.

★ 18 gingersnaps
1 cup sugar
2 ounces (¼ cup) melted
   butter
1 quart vanilla ice cream
1 cup mashed cooked
   pumpkin, fresh or canned

1 teaspoon grated fresh
   gingerroot or ½ teaspoon
   ground
1 teaspoon ground cinnamon
½ teaspoon ground cloves
½ teaspoon grated nutmeg
½ cup heavy cream, whipped
½ cup chopped pecans

Crush gingersnaps. Combine with ½ cup sugar and the melted butter. Press into the bottom and sides of a 9-inch pie plate. Chill. Soften ice cream. Beat until smooth. Spread on crumb base. Freeze until firm. Mix pumpkin with remaining ½ cup sugar and the spices. Fold in whipped cream. Smooth over ice cream. Freeze until firm. Sprinkle with nuts. Yield: 8 servings.

CHOCOLATE CREAM SQUARES

1 package (12 oz.) semisweet
   chocolate bits
1 tablespoon milk
4 eggs, separated
2 tablespoons confectioners'
   sugar

1 cup chopped nuts
1 cup heavy cream, whipped
★ 1 package (12 oz.) vanilla or
   chocolate wafers, crushed

Melt chocolate bits with milk in the top part of a double boiler over hot water. Beat egg yolks, one at a time, into hot chocolate, beating well after each addition. Add sugar and nuts. Cool. Beat egg whites until stiff. Fold into chocolate mixture. Fold in whipped cream. Sprinkle half of the wafer crumbs in the bottom of an 8-inch-square pan. Pour chocolate cream carefully over crumbs. Sprinkle with remaining crumbs. Chill for at least 24 hours, preferably 48. Cut into squares and serve. Yield: 8 servings.

ICE-CREAM SQUARES

There is no dessert better than ice cream, especially when you combine it with delicious ingredients.

★ 1 package (12 oz.) vanilla or
   chocolate wafers, crushed
¼ pound (½ cup) butter
2 ounces unsweetened
   chocolate
1½ cups sifted confectioners'
   sugar

3 eggs, separated
1 teaspoon vanilla extract
1 cup chopped nuts
½ gallon vanilla ice cream,
   softened

Grease a 13 x 9 x 2 inch pan heavily with butter or margarine. Sprinkle half the crumbs over the bottom evenly. Combine ¼ pound (½ cup) butter and chocolate in the top part of a double boiler. Heat over boiling water until chocolate is melted. Beat in sugar. Add egg yolks, one at a time, beating well after each addition. Beat in vanilla. Beat egg whites until stiff. Stir in a large spoonful. Fold in remaining whites. Pour mixture over crumbs. Sprinkle with nuts. Freeze until firm. Spread with softened ice cream. Sprinkle with remaining crumbs. Freeze until firm. Cut into 3-inch squares. Yield: 12 servings.

GRAHAM CRACKER CRUST

★ 20 graham crackers
         or
★ 2 cups packaged graham-
   cracker crumbs

¼ cup sugar
2⅔ ounces (⅓ cup) melted
   butter or margarine

If using crackers roll between 2 sheets of waxed paper to make crumbs. Pour crumbs into a bowl and mix well with sugar and melted butter or margarine. Press into a greased 9-inch pie plate. Place in a preheated 350° F. oven for 7 minutes. Cool and fill.

Note: Ground macaroons, gingersnaps or wheat cereals may be substituted in the crust recipe. Use whatever coupon is available.

CHOCOLATE MERINGUE PIE

Of all the desserts I served in my restaurant days, this was easily the most popular. People would phone to see whether it was on the menu before reserving a table. It was also my busy-day recipe, so easy and so foolproof.

3 egg whites, at room
  temperature
1 cup granulated sugar
½ tablespoon baking powder
★ 17 unsalted soda crackers
½ cup finely chopped nuts

2 teaspoons vanilla extract
1 jar (12 oz.) chocolate fudge
  topping
1 cup heavy cream
2 tablespoons confectioners'
  sugar

Beat egg whites until soft peaks form. Gradually beat in granulated sugar. Beat in baking powder and continue to beat until very stiff. Crush 14 of the soda crackers and fold into the meringue along with nuts and 1 teaspoon vanilla. Crush remaining 3 soda crackers and sprinkle crumbs in the bottom of a 9-inch pie plate. Smooth meringue over the crumb layer and up the sides of the pie plate. Place in a preheated 350° F. oven and bake for 25 minutes. Cool. Spread fudge sauce over top of meringue. Beat the cream until stiff, then sweeten with confectioners' sugar and flavor with remaining vanilla. Garnish the pie. Yield: 8 to 10 servings.

SNOWBALLS

This is a pretty dessert to serve at Christmastime. Top each snowball with a sprig of holly.

12 ounces (¾ lb.) unsalted
  butter
1½ cups sugar
2 eggs, separated
1 cup crushed pineapple, very
  well drained
1 cup chopped nuts
dash salt

★ 48 vanilla wafers, 2 inches in
  diameter
4 egg whites, at room
  temperature
⅛ teaspoon cream of tartar
dash of salt
¼ cup water
3 ounces cream cheese
2 cups moist flaked coconut

Cream ¼ pound (4 oz.) butter and ½ cup sugar. Add 2 egg yolks, pineapple and nuts. Beat 2 egg whites with salt until stiff. Fold into pineapple mixture. Spread between 6 wafers, stacking them into 8 separate bundles. Refrigerate overnight.

Beat remaining 4 egg whites until stiff. Set aside. Place 1 cup sugar, the cream of tartar, salt and water in a saucepan. Bring to a rolling boil and cook until syrup registers 240° F. on a candy thermometer. Pour over stiffly beaten egg whites very slowly, beating constantly. Continue to beat until cooled. Refrigerate this meringue until cold. Soften remaining butter. Beat the ½ pound sweet butter · and cream cheese, a bit at a time, into the cold meringue. Spread each bundle of filled wafers with this frosting. Roll in coconut and serve. Yield: 8 servings.

9 COUPONS FOR ICE CREAMS AND SHERBETS

Everyone loves frozen sweets, and we're including in this category bulk ice creams and sherbets, popsicles, ice cream on a stick, sandwiches, bars, etc. Bars, pops and sticks really don't need embellishment. Bulk ice creams and sherbets, in conjunction with other ingredients, make wonderful dessert specialties. Their greatest contribution is their versatility and the fact that they can be made ahead. To have the dessert in the freezer is a great boon when you're under pressure preparing for a party. Most ice creams or sherbet dishes will keep in the freezer for 3 to 5 months. Do not allow them to melt and then refreeze; this results in a grainy texture with ice crystals throughout.

The variations on frozen sweets can be endless, so I've chosen a select few. They are very festive and can be decorated to commemorate any holiday of your choice. A sprig of holly on the Raspberry Bombe (p. 120) turns daily fare into Christmas fare. Sprinkle nuts on the ends and top of the Ice-Cream Log (p. 119) and you'll have a winter log for midwinter parties. Tiny cinnamon hearts will decorate any one of these confections for St. Valentine's Day. Ingenuity is the keynote when entertaining. If you wish, just mix layers of ice creams and sherbets in different colors and freeze to make a multicolored mold. Serve with Cocoa Glaze (p. 157) and you have an instant dessert. The recipes in this section take a little more effort than that but are well worth the time. They look spectacular and they taste delicious.

ICE CREAM WITH ZABAGLIONE SAUCE

Italy contributed this frothy custard to the world's cuisine. It makes an excellent sauce, but can be served as a dessert by itself.

6 egg yolks
⅓ cup sugar

4 ounces Marsala wine
★ 4 scoops of vanilla ice cream

Place egg yolks and sugar in the top part of a double boiler. Beat over hot water, adding Marsala, 1 tablespoon at a time, until the mixture is very thick and foamy. Place ice cream in sherbet glasses. Pour zabaglione over top and serve at once. Yield: 4 servings.

Note: Zabaglione may be poured still warm into sherbet glasses without any ice cream and served at once. Some people use rum instead of Marsala, but Marsala wine is the traditional choice.

CHOCOLATE MOUSSE MOLD

★ 3 pints chocolate-chip ice
   cream
4 ounces semisweet chocolate
2 teaspoons instant coffee
   powder

2 tablespoons boiling water
4 eggs, separated
⅓ cup sugar
1 teaspoon vanilla extract
dash of salt

Line a 2-quart mold with a layer of ice cream, making a shell ½ inch thick. Place in the freezer. Melt chocolate over hot water. Dissolve coffee in boiling water and stir into chocolate; mix well. Beat egg yolks until thick and very pale in color. Beat in sugar until a ribbon forms (see Note 2, p. 150). Beat in melted chocolate and vanilla.

Beat egg whites with salt until stiff but not dry. Stir one quarter of egg whites into chocolate mixture. Fold in remaining whites. Place in refrigerator to thicken for 2 hours or more. Turn into cavity of ice-cream mold. Freeze until firm. Smooth a ½-inch layer of ice cream over top. Freeze until firm. Unmold and serve with Cocoa Glaze (p. 157). Yield: 10 servings.

Note: Eliminating the ice cream, you have a classic *mousse au chocolat.* It freezes very well, but traditionally is served unfrozen in individual soufflé dishes or glass coupes.

ICE-CREAM LOG

Try this for something different next time you entertain. You will need a 48-ounce juice can, well washed, dried and chilled.

★ 1 pint vanilla ice cream, softened
★ 1 pint chocolate ice cream, softened
★ 1 quart lime sherbet
2 cups heavy cream

¼ cup confectioners' sugar
1 teaspoon vanilla extract
shaved chocolate (see Comment, p. 107)

Smooth the vanilla ice cream evenly around insides of the prepared can, forming a shell ½ inch deep. Freeze until solid. Smooth chocolate ice cream in a ½-inch layer inside vanilla ice cream. Freeze solid. Fill cavity with lime sherbet. Freeze solid. Dip a long knife in hot water. Slip it down sides of can to release the dessert. Remove bottom of can with a can opener. Push mold through bottom of can. Place on a long board or dessert dish. Beat cream with confectioners' sugar and vanilla until stiff. Frost roll with whipped cream. Garnish with shaved chocolate. (Leftover ice cream can be refrozen.) Yield: 8 servings.

RASPBERRY BOMBE

This beautiful dessert tastes as good as it looks. The best part is the convenience of making it ahead and having it in the freezer when needed.

2 cups heavy cream
¼ cup confectioners' sugar
1 teaspoon vanilla extract

½ cup blanched almonds, finely chopped
★ 1½ quarts raspberry sherbet
Raspberry Sauce (recipe follows)

Whip heavy cream with sugar and vanilla until stiff. Fold in almonds. Wet a 2½-quart mold and line with two thirds of the cream. Freeze until firm. Fill cavity with sherbet. Freeze until firm. Smooth remaining whipped cream over top. Freeze until firm. Dip mold into hot water, count to 10, place a serving plate over top, and quickly invert. Blot up any melted cream with paper toweling. Pour raspberry sauce over top and serve. Yield: 8 to 10 servings.

Raspberry Sauce

1 package (9 oz.) frozen raspberries
2 tablespoons currant jelly

1 teaspoon arrowroot or 1 tablespoon cornstarch (see Note)
¼ cup water
2 tablespoons Kirschwasser

Place raspberries and currant jelly in a small saucepan. Heat until jelly melts. Dissolve arrowroot or cornstarch in ¼ cup water and stir into hot sauce. When thickened and clear, stir in Kirschwasser. Cool then chill. Pour over bombe. Yield: 1½ cups.

Note: Arrowroot is expensive, but much less is needed to do the job compared to cornstarch. It also gives a lighter quality to the sauces than cornstarch does.

10 COUPONS FOR JAMS, JELLIES, HONEY, PEANUT BUTTER, MARMALADE AND SYRUPS

Coupons are regularly offered for items in this category. There are so many more inventive things one can do than just spread them over bread. Many main-course dishes are enhanced with the addition of a sweet. Rich dishes such as duck, goose, lamb and pork definitely benefit from the tart sweetness of apricot or currant glaze. Marmalade makes a fast *"à l'orange"* sauce, eliminating the preparation of the traditional sauce. Honey enriches any number of dishes with a special flavor.

This chapter includes recipes for appetizers and main-course dishes and for baked goods and desserts. If a recipe calls for strawberry jam, raspberry or plum preserves may be substituted. Currant jelly and apricot preserves are interchangeable in tartness if not in taste. If you wish to substitute peach jam for any of these, add 1 or 2 tablespoons of lemon or lime juice for added tartness. I would not recommend substituting grape jelly for currant as grape has a distinctive flavor and color that does not harmonize well. Marmalade is in a class by itself; when it is made from bitter Valencia oranges, it will have a decidedly more bitter taste than when made with sweet oranges. Peanut butters come smooth and chunky; use whichever one you prefer.

APPETIZERS AND MAIN-COURSE DISHES

Appetizers by nature should not be sweet but pungent and appetite-inducing. Sugar is appetite reducing, so it is better not to offer sweet dishes before a meal. Both appetizer and soup use peanut butter rather than any sweet ingredient.

STUFFED CELERY APPETIZER

This recipe is a variation on a theme for all those peanut lovers.

3 ounces cream cheese, at
   room temperature
1 tablespoon grated onion
2 teaspoons chili sauce
★ 3 tablespoons peanut butter

5 pitted ripe olives, chopped
10 to 12 celery ribs, cut into
   2½-inch lengths
chopped unsalted peanuts

Mash cream cheese. Add onion, chili sauce, peanut butter and olives. Mix well. Spread on celery lengths. Sprinkle with chopped peanuts. Yield: 36 pieces.

HONEY-GLAZED CHICKEN

My older son loves this dish. It is quick and easy to prepare for entertaining.

1 broiler-fryer chicken, 3
   pounds
2 tablespoons oil

★ ¼ cup honey
¼ cup prepared Dijon mustard
2 tablespoons lemon juice

Cut chicken into serving portions. Heat oil in a skillet and brown chicken quickly on all sides. Arrange pieces in a single layer in a shallow baking pan. Mix honey, mustard and lemon juice, and pour over chicken. Bake in a preheated 350° F. oven for 30 minutes. Turn, brush with pan juice and bake for another 20 minutes. Yield: 3 servings.

QUICK DUCK À L'ORANGE

This is the easiest and fastest way to do duck that I know of, but start it well ahead of time as the duck must cool after the first roasting. Be sure the duck is very crispy before serving (see Comment, p. 148).

1 duck, 4 to 5 pounds
Marmalade Sauce (recipe follows)
salt and pepper

If duck is frozen let it defrost, still wrapped, in the refrigerator for 48 hours. Wash duck inside and out, and pat dry. Sprinkle liberally with salt and pepper inside and out. Prick surface with a fork. Place on a rack and roast in a preheated 350° F. oven for 1½ hours. Remove from oven, cool completely, and cut each breast into 2 portions and each thigh into 2 portions, forming 8 small pieces. Place the portions on a rack in a shallow baking dish. Bake in the oven for 30 minutes before serving. Brush with marmalade sauce about 15 minutes before removing from the oven. Yield: 4 servings.

Marmalade Sauce

★ 1 jar (10 oz.) marmalade
juice of 1 lemon
¼ cup orange juice
½ teaspoon salt

freshly ground pepper
2 tablespoons duck fat
2 tablespoons Marsala wine

Mix marmalade, lemon and orange juices and salt and pepper to taste. Heat, stirring, until marmalade has melted. Stir in duck fat and wine. Brush over the duck pieces. Yield: approximately 1½ cups.

SOUTHERN PEANUT SOUP

Peanut butter in soup may be unfamiliar, but it is a Southern favorite. Try it; you will be amazed how good it tastes. It is also very nutritious.

1 large onion, chopped
2 celery ribs, chopped
2 ounces (4 tablespoons)
    butter or margarine
2 tablespoons flour

3 cups beef broth, canned or
    instant, boiling
★ ½ cup peanut butter
salt and freshly ground pepper
2 tablespoons chopped
    unsalted peanuts (optional)

Sauté onion and celery in butter or margarine in a 2½-quart saucepan. Sprinkle with flour and cook, stirring constantly for 2 to 3 minutes. Off the heat, beat in boiling broth. Cover and simmer, stirring occasionally, for 30 minutes. Stir in peanut butter, and salt and pepper to taste. Serve with a sprinkling of chopped nuts if desired. Yield: 4 to 6 servings.

CHICKEN PARISIENNE

This is a fine dish for entertaining. Preparation can be done well ahead, with the final baking done just before serving.

2 pounds chicken breasts,
    boned
flour for dredging
2 ounces (4 tablespoons)
    butter or margarine
1 teaspoon tomato paste
4 tablespoons flour
2 cups chicken broth, canned,
    fresh or instant, boiling

1 cup commercial sour cream,
    at room temperature (see
    Note)
salt and pepper
★ 1 tablespoon currant jelly
½ cup grated Parmesan
    cheese

Roll chicken breasts in flour. Shake to remove excess flour. Heat butter or margarine to sizzling in a skillet. Brown breasts on each side. Lay pieces in a single layer in an ovenproof dish, attractive enough to serve in. Set aside.

Add tomato paste and flour to the skillet chicken was browned in. Cook, stirring, for 2 to 3 minutes. Off the heat, beat in the boiling broth with a wire whisk. Beat in sour cream, salt and pepper to taste and currant jelly. Cook over low heat, stirring, until jelly melts. Add ¼ cup cheese and cook until cheese is incorporated. Pour this sauce over chicken. Sprinkle remaining cheese on top. Bake in a pre-heated 350° F. oven for 20 minutes. Run under the broiler for 2 to 3 minutes, or until topping is browned. Serve at once. Yield: 4 servings.

Note: Sour cream must be at room temperature before being stirred into a hot sauce. If sour cream is taken directly from refrigerator and added, icy cold, to a hot sauce, it will separate and curdle.

STEAK TERIYAKI

Flank steak is comparatively reasonable in cost, however, it seems to be a matter of luck whether it is tender or not. Marinating it, then slicing it across the grain in paper-thin diagonal slices should give good results. Bear in mind that flank steak should be decidedly pink in the middle, and this recipe calls for marinating for 6 to 8 hours.

1 garlic clove, crushed	2 tablespoons vinegar
4 scallions, chopped	1 ounce sherry
½ cup salad oil	1 tablespoon freshly grated
¼ cup soy sauce	gingerroot
★ ¼ cup honey	2 pounds trimmed beef flank steak

Mix first 8 ingredients together. Pour over steak and marinate, turning meat often, for 6 to 8 hours. Heat broiler. Pat meat dry with paper toweling. Broil for 6 to 8 minutes on one side. Turn and broil for 5 minutes on second side. Slice as suggested. Yield: 4 servings.

SWEET-AND-SOUR CHINESE PORK

This dish tastes equally good using either loin or tenderloin. The loin must be very well trimmed of all fat before marinating. Tenderloins are not easy to find, but they can usually be purchased from a private butcher or a pork shop. Be sure to start this 4 to 6 hours before you intend to serve it.

4 pounds loin or tenderloin of
   pork
1 garlic clove
2 ounces sherry
½ cup soy sauce

2 tablespoons sugar
1 teaspoon salt
freshly ground pepper
1 teaspoon ground cinnamon
Plum Sauce (recipe follows)

Trim loin of most of its fat. Pierce surface at 2-inch intervals with a sharp knife. Cut garlic into slivers and force a sliver into each slash. Mix sherry, soy sauce, sugar, salt, pepper to taste and cinnamon. Pour over meat and marinate for 4 to 6 hours. Pat dry. Place pork on a rack in a shallow roasting pan. Roast in a preheated 325° F. oven for 30 minutes to the pound. Serve with plum sauce. Yield: 8 servings.

Plum Sauce

½ cup and 2 tablespoons
   orange juice
1½ cups dry white wine
★ ½ jar (10-oz. size) Duck Sauce
★ 2 tablespoons currant jelly

1 tablespoon freshly grated
   gingerroot, or 1 teaspoon
   ground ginger
★ 1 tablespoon honey
1 tablespoon cornstarch

Mix ½ cup orange juice and next 5 ingredients together. Bring to a boil and simmer, stirring, until currant jelly melts. Dissolve cornstarch in 2 tablespoons orange juice. Stir into boiling sauce. Cook until clear and thick. Yield: 2 cups sauce.

Microwave Cooking: Marinate meat as described. Pat dry. Place in ceramic dish, covered with plastic wrap, and microwave on "medium" setting for 13 to 15 minutes per pound. Remove from oven. Mix ingredients for plum sauce in a small ceramic or glass bowl.

Place in oven on "high" setting. Microwave for 3 minutes. Stir. If not thickened, return to oven and cook for another 3 minutes. Serve sauce with pork.

ROAST GOOSE WITH HONEY GLAZE

Fruit Stuffing (recipe follows)
1 goose, 10 to 12 pounds
salt and pepper
★ 1 cup honey

juice of 1 lemon
1 tablespoon soy sauce
1 teaspoon ground ginger

Prepare fruit stuffing. Wash inside cavity of goose. Sprinkle cavity liberally with salt and pepper. Pack cavity and neck loosely with stuffing. Skewer or stitch openings closed. Truss goose, tieing legs and wings together with cord. Place goose, breast side down, on a rack in a shallow pan. Bake in a preheated 325° F. oven for 3 hours. Turn goose breast side up. Brush liberally with a mixture of the honey, lemon juice, soy sauce and ginger. Bake for another 2 hours, basting with the honey mixture every 15 minutes. Remove from oven; cut trussing cords; allow goose to rest for 15 minutes. Carve and serve. Yield: 8 servings.

Fruit Stuffing

4 firm apples
1 cup pitted prunes
1 onion, chopped
3 celery ribs, chopped
2 ounces (4 tablespoons)
    butter or margarine

2 cups soft bread crumbs
1 teaspoon salt
freshly ground pepper
1 teaspoon poultry seasoning

Peel, core, and chop apples. Chop prunes. Sauté onion and celery in butter or margarine until limp. Add apples and prunes. Sauté for 2 to 3 minutes longer. Remove from heat and toss with remaining ingredients. Yield: stuffing for a 10- to 12-pound goose or 2 ducks, 4 pounds each.

SAUERBRATEN

Serve this German dinner with sauerkraut and potato pancakes, with a strudel for dessert. But be sure to start marinating the meat 3 days ahead as explained in the instructions. It's worth the wait!

5 pounds beef bottom round or rump roast
2 celery ribs, chopped
10 small white onions (see Note 1)
1 pound mushrooms, trimmed (see Note 2)
1 green pepper, seeded and chopped
4 carrots, scraped and cut into ¼-inch circles

1 teaspoon salt
freshly ground pepper
2 cups red wine
★ ½ cup red currant jelly
½ cup vinegar
1 bay leaf
2 whole cloves
12 gingersnaps
2 teaspoons instant beef base powder, or 2 bouillon cubes

Trim fat from meat and discard. Place meat in a Dutch oven. Surround with vegetables. Salt and pepper liberally. Place wine and jelly in a saucepan; heat until jelly melts, then pour over meat and vegetables. Add vinegar, bay leaf and cloves. Marinate in refrigerator for 3 days, turning regularly.

Remove beef from Dutch oven. Pat dry on paper toweling. Brown on all sides in hot oil in a skillet. Add 6 gingersnaps to marinade. Return meat to Dutch oven, and bring liquid to a boil on top of the stove. Cover. Braise in a preheated 350° F. oven for 2 hours (see Comment).

Remove meat from liquid. Add 6 more gingersnaps and the beef base to sauce. Gingersnaps will dissolve in hot liquid and act as a thickening agent. Slice meat. If not tender to your taste, return to the sauce and cook until fork tender. Yield: 10 servings.

Note 1: Peel small white onions and remove root end. Cut a cross in root end about ¼ inch deep. This keeps insides of onion from popping out during cooking period.

Note 2: Present-day mushrooms do not need peeling or washing.

They are grown under carefully supervised conditions. Any dirt should be wiped off with a damp cloth. Like all fungi, mushrooms absorb liquid. If you soak them in water, you dilute the taste.

Comment: Braise means to cook slowly in some liquid after an initial process of browning in oil.

Microwave Cooking: Place meat, after browning, in a glass or ceramic dish. Add marinade and gingersnaps. Cover with plastic wrap. Microwave on "medium" setting for 1 hour. Proceed with basic recipe. After adding final gingersnaps, microwave for 1 minute before serving.

BAKED GOODS AND DESSERTS

The following recipes are specialties of their kind and are well worth the effort.

HONEY-KAHLÚA MOLD

I served this very rich dessert when I was a restaurateur. Use Kahlúa or your own homemade coffee liqueur.

6 eggs yolks
★ ½ cup honey
2 cups heavy cream

2 ounces Kahlúa, or Coffee
Liqueur (p. 179)
shaved chocolate (p. 107)

Beat egg yolks with honey. Pour into the top part of a double boiler over hot water and cook, stirring, until thick. Cool completely. Beat cream with Kahlúa until stiff, and fold into egg mixture. Turn into a 1½-quart mold and freeze.

Dip mold into hot water, count to 10, and invert on a serving plate. Garnish with shaved chocolate. Yield: 8 to 10 servings.

FILLED DESSERT CRÊPES WITH APRICOT SAUCE

Make both crêpes and sauce ahead and heat at the last moment.

1⅓ cups milk	1 tablespoon sugar
3 eggs	1 ounce (2 tablespoons)
1½ cup all-purpose flour	melted margarine

Place milk and eggs in a bowl. Beat well. Beat in remaining ingredients. Allow batter to rest for 2 hours. Make crêpes according to instructions on page 177. Yield: 16 crêpes.

Apricot-Cheese Filling

8 ounces cream cheese, softened	★ ¼ cup honey
	1 teaspoon vanilla extract
2 ounces butter (4 tablespoons), softened	1 can (1 lb.) pitted whole apricots, well drained

Mix cheese, butter, honey and vanilla very well. Spread each crêpe with some of this mixture. Lay 2 whole apricots down the middle of each crêpe. Roll up crêpes and lay them, seam side down, in a shallow baking pan. Bake in a preheated 350° F. oven for 10 minutes. Serve with apricot sauce. Yield: 8 servings, 2 crêpes each.

Apricot Sauce

★ ⅔ cup apricot preserves	1½ teaspoons grated lemon rind
⅓ cup orange juice	
1 ounce (2 tablespoons) butter	★ 2 tablespoons honey
2 tablespoons lemon juice	

Combine all ingredients in a small saucepan. Heat, stirring, until apricot preserves melt and sauce is smooth. Yield: 1½ cups.

Microwave Cooking: Lay filled crêpes in a glass or ceramic serving dish. Place in oven on "medium" setting and microwave for 6 to 7 minutes, or until heated through. Combine all sauce ingredients in an attractive serving dish or jug. Microwave on "medium" setting for 3 to 4 minutes.

LINZERTORTE

This rich Austrian dessert is a specialty of Linz. Austrians are masters of dessert-making. Be prepared to gain several pounds if you visit Vienna. The city boasts many fine Konditereien, laden with glorious desserts.

2 cups all-purpose flour, sifted
pinch of salt
⅓ cup sugar
1 teaspoon ground cinnamon
1½ cups ground blanched
   almonds (see p. 150)

6 ounces (¾ cup) sweet butter
2 eggs, lightly beaten
1 ounce rum or brandy
★ 2 cups good raspberry jam
   confectioners' sugar

Sift flour, salt, sugar and cinnamon into a bowl. Add ground almonds and mix well. Cut in butter. Add eggs and liquor, stirring until dough leaves sides of bowl. Form into a ball. Chill thoroughly. Cut into halves. Roll one half out on a floured board. Line a 10-inch quiche pan with this pastry (see Note). Spread 1½ cups jam over the pastry. Roll out remaining pastry and form a lattice over top of the tart. Bake in a 325° F. oven for 50 to 60 minutes, or until a toothpick inserted in the middle comes out clean. Fill spaces between lattice strips with remaining jam. Cool. Dust with confectioners' sugar just before serving. Yield: 8 to 10 servings.

Note: A "quiche" pan or dish is about 1 inch deep with a diameter varying from 7 inches to 10 inches. Some quiche pans have a removable bottom. To serve, remove the side rim, leaving the quiche resting on the bottom. However, French china quiche dishes or tart pans are used for serving as well as baking.

SACHERTORTE

This cake was invented by a chef at the Viennese Hotel Sacher. It is traditionally served with a large dollop of whipped cream on the side.

¼ pound (½ cup) margarine
1 cup sugar
6 egg yolks
6 ounces semisweet chocolate, melted and cooled
1 cup sifted flour (see p. 159)
2 tablespoons cocoa powder

8 egg whites, at room temperature
½ teaspoon cream of tartar
★ ½ jar (10-oz. size) currant jelly (see Note)
Chocolate Glaze (recipe follows)

Butter a 10-inch springform pan. Line with wax paper and butter the paper. Cream margarine and ½ cup sugar well. Add egg yolks and beat until fluffy. Stir in cooled melted chocolate. Sift flour and cocoa together 3 times. Beat egg whites until foamy. Beat in cream of tartar and remaining ½ cup sugar, and continue to beat until meringue is stiff but not dry. Stir a large tablespoon of egg whites into yolk mixture. Fold in one quarter of the flour mixture. Continue folding in alternate portions of egg whites and flour until all is incorporated. Spoon into the prepared pan. Bake in a preheated 350° F. oven for 40 minutes, or until cake begins to shrink from sides of pan and springs back when pressed on the surface with a fingertip.

Cool cake on a rack. Slice horizontally into halves (see Note, p. 95). Melt currant jelly over low heat. Brush cake layers with melted jelly, then reassemble and brush all over outside surfaces with melted jelly. Let jelly set. Pour chocolate glaze over cake. Yield: 12 servings.

Chocolate Glaze

6 ounces semisweet chocolate
¾ cup heavy cream
½ cup sugar

★ 2 teaspoons corn syrup
1½ ounces (3 tablespoons) butter

Cook chocolate, cream, sugar and syrup over low heat, stirring constantly, for 10 minutes. Beat in butter. Beat glaze until thick and cool. Pour over cake.

Note: Apricot preserves may be substituted for currant jelly, and apricot glaze is used in the original Viennese recipe. However, I prefer to use currant jelly as a glaze for dark-colored desserts and apricot glaze for light-colored desserts.

APPLE STRUDEL

The addition of apricot jam to the strudel filling makes this dessert spectacular.

6 sheets of fillo dough (see
  Note, p. 56)
4 ounces (½ cup) melted
  butter or margarine
½ cup fine dry bread crumbs
6 large cooking apples

1 cup raisins or currants
¾ cup packed brown sugar
1 teaspoon ground cinnamon
★ ½ jar (12-oz. jar) apricot
  preserves

Lay 1 sheet of fillo dough on a clean dish towel. Brush with melted butter or margarine and sprinkle with bread crumbs. Lay another sheet of fillo on top of this and repeat. Continue until all sheets of dough are piled together, buttered and sprinkled with crumbs. Peel, core and chop apples. Mix with raisins or currants. Toss with brown sugar and cinnamon. Spread prepared pastry with apricot preserves. Lay apple mixture on top of one long edge of the fillo dough. Using the dish towel to help, roll up the sheets of dough to enclose apple filling. Lay strudel, seam side down, on a jellyroll pan. Brush with remaining melted butter or margarine. Bake in a preheated 350° F. oven for 1 hour, or until apples are soft and strudel is browned. Yield: 8 servings.

11
COUPONS FOR PANCAKES AND BREADS

Commercially prepared mixes, used in making breads, pancakes, biscuits, rolls, etc., are the theme of this chapter. Frozen and refrigerated doughs are also included. These are convenience foods that save hours of preparation. They are less economical and less satisfying than making your own baked goods from scratch, but for a busy housewife or working person, the time saved is well worth the extra cost. I still feel pre-preparation costs something in taste, but many of these items are good substitutes for your own. The other advantage of these products is that they always work successfully. Carefully followed instructions create foolproof results.

Coupons covering most of these items are issued regularly. Good use of this chapter can be made if you glance at the recipes every time a coupon appears. Well utilized, these products can help stretch budgets, but care should be taken to balance the meal adequately when serving high-carbohydrate items. Do not serve starches such as potatoes, rice or noodles when using breads, biscuits or pancakes as part of the menu. A good green vegetable, tossed fresh salad and fruity dessert complement such a menu. If the dessert is heavy, serve it with a light supper or luncheon dish. Weigh one course against another and your meals will get high marks for health and nutrition. Recipes in this chapter include canapés, appetizers and main-course dishes and pancakes, waffles and desserts.

APPETIZERS, ONE BREAD AND MAIN-COURSE DISHES

COCKTAIL FRANKFURTERS

Make this with sausages if you prefer. Sauté sausages until all fat is rendered before baking. Fingers of salami or bologna can also be substituted.

★ 1 can (7½ oz.) refrigerator
   biscuits
36 cocktail frankfurters,
   cooked

2 egg yolks, beaten with ¼ cup
   water
poppy seeds
prepared Dijon mustard

Cut each biscuit into 4 pieces. Roll each piece into a strip long enough to encircle a frankfurter, leaving ends uncovered. Roll a strip around each frankfurter and secure with a toothpick. Brush with egg wash. Lay in a single layer on a greased cookie sheet. Sprinkle with poppy seeds. Bake in a preheated 425° F. oven for 10 minutes. Serve around an attractive dish filled with Dijon mustard. Yield: 36 servings.

CHEESE TOMATO BITS

This is like a tiny bite-size pizza. The cheese, tomato and orégano make this hot canapé very popular.

★ 2 cups biscuit mix
⅔ cup milk
1 can (6 oz.) tomato paste
2 garlic cloves, crushed
2 tablespoons red wine

¼ pound mozzarella cheese, shredded
1 can (2 oz.) anchovy fillets
grated Parmesan cheese
crumbled dried orégano

Blend biscuit mix with milk to make a stiff dough. Roll out ¼ inch thick on a floured board. Cut into 1½-inch rounds with a floured glass or biscuit cutter. Mix tomato paste, garlic and wine. Spread each biscuit with some of this mixture. Top with a sprinkling of shredded mozzarella. Lay a small piece of anchovy over this. Sprinkle with Parmesan cheese and orégano. Bake in a preheated 450° F. oven for 10 minutes. Yield: 24 to 30 canapés.

SWEETBREAD AND MUSHROOM HORS-D'OEUVRE

This hors-d'oeuvre is tricky to make, but when you see the elegant results you will agree it was well worth the effort.

★ 1 package (12 oz.) 8 French rolls
1 pound veal sweetbreads
1 tablespoon vinegar
salt
½ pound mushrooms
4 ounces (8 tablespoons) butter
pepper
3 shallots, chopped

1 garlic clove, crushed
1 teaspoon dried, crushed basil or 1 tablespoon minced fresh
4 tablespoons flour
1½ cups beef broth, canned or instant, boiling
4 ounces sherry
3 tablespoons chopped fresh parsley

Bake rolls according to package instructions. Cut off the top quarter of each roll. Scoop out insides, leaving a ¼-inch shell (use top and insides for making bread crumbs). Set bread shells aside.

Soak sweetbreads in water to cover for 1 hour. Drain. Bring 1 quart water to a boil. Add vinegar and 1 teaspoon salt. Drop sweetbreads into the acidulated water and simmer for 20 minutes. Drain and immediately plunge sweetbreads into ice water. Remove membrane and tubes. Cut sweetbreads into small pieces. Set aside.

Slice mushrooms and sauté in 1 ounce (2 tablespoons) butter. Add another ounce (2 tablespoons) of butter and sauté sweetbreads for 5 minutes, stirring. Season with salt and pepper to taste. Set aside.

Sauté shallots in remaining butter in a 2-quart saucepan for 2 to 3 minutes. Add garlic and basil. Sauté for 1 to 2 minutes, stirring. Sprinkle with flour and cook, stirring, for 2 to 3 minutes. Off the heat, beat in the boiling broth. Return to the heat and cook for 5 minutes. Stir in sherry, 1 teaspoon salt, pepper to taste and parsley. Add sweetbreads and mushrooms to the sauce. Heat thoroughly. Bake bread shells in a preheated 350° F. oven for 5 minutes. Fill with hot sweetbread mixture and serve at once. Yield: 8 servings.

GARLIC BREAD

This recipe makes very good garlic bread. Make well ahead and pop on the oven 20 minutes before serving.

★ 1 ready-to-bake loaf of French bread
½ pound butter or margarine, at room temperature

3 garlic cloves, crushed
1 teaspoon crumbled dried orégano

Slice bread almost, but not quite, through into 1-inch slices. Mash butter or margarine with garlic and orégano. Spread butter between slices and across top of the loaf. Wrap in aluminum foil, leaving top exposed. Bake in a preheated 400° F. oven for 20 minutes. Serve at once. Yield: 4 to 6 servings.

MEAT LOAF EN CROÛTE

This is an excellent way to stretch 1 pound of ground beef.

1 pound ground or chopped
  beef
1 teaspoon salt
freshly ground pepper
1 onion, minced
1 egg
2 cups soft bread crumbs

¾ cup grated Cheddar cheese
1 cup milk
★ 1 recipe biscuit dough made
  from mix, using 2 cups mix
  and ⅔ cup milk
1 egg yolk, beaten with 1
  tablespoon water

Mix beef with salt, pepper to taste, onion, egg, bread crumbs, cheese and enough milk to bind. Roll out biscuit dough on a floured board to ¼-inch thickness. Shape meat into a loaf down the middle of the biscuit dough. Fold edges of dough over loaf; pinch edges together. Place loaf, fold side down, on a greased baking pan. Brush all over with egg wash. Bake in a preheated 450° F. oven for 15 minutes. Reduce heat to 350° F. and bake for another 30 minutes. Remove from oven. Allow to rest for 10 minutes, then cut into 1-inch slices to serve. Yield: 8 servings.

CHICKEN AND OYSTER PIE WITH BISCUITS

This is a great way to use leftover chicken or turkey. The oysters give it a dressed-up quality.

1 onion, chopped
1 celery rib, chopped
1 garlic clove, chopped
3 ounces (6 tablespoons)
  butter
4 tablespoons flour
1½ cups chicken broth, boiling
½ cup cream, scalded
1 teaspoon salt

freshly ground pepper
1 teaspoon paprika
½ pound mushrooms, sliced
1 pint shucked oysters,
  drained
2 cups diced cooked chicken
  or turkey
★ 1 can (7½ oz.) refrigerator
  biscuits

Sauté onion, celery and garlic in 2 ounces (4 tablespoons) butter until onion is limp but not browned. Sprinkle with flour and cook, stirring, for 2 to 3 minutes. Off the heat, add boiling broth all at once, beating vigorously with a wire whisk. Return to heat and cook for 2 to 3 minutes. Add cream, salt, pepper to taste and paprika. Sauté mushrooms in remaining 1 ounce (2 tablespoons) butter for 5 minutes. Scrape into sauce. Add oysters and chicken. Pour into an 8-cup casserole. Arrange biscuits on top of casserole. Bake in a preheated 400° F. oven for 20 minutes, or until biscuits are puffed and brown. Yield: 6 servings.

MOCK CRÊPE LUNCHEON

The combination of very thin pancakes, ham and cheese makes a hearty luncheon main dish. Make well ahead and heat in the oven or, better still, in a microwave oven. Kids love this meal with a bowl of soup.

★ 1 cup packaged pancake mix
1½ cups liquid skim milk
1 large egg
1 tablespoon oil
¼ pound (½ cup) melted
   margarine

½ pound very thin slices of
   ham
½ pound very thin slices of
   American or Cheddar
   cheese

Beat pancake mix with milk, egg and oil. Allow to stand for 20 minutes. Heat a 6-inch skillet. Brush with melted margarine. Pour 3 tablespoons batter into pan and swirl to coat bottom. Allow to set. Flip over the pancake and cook on the other side. Set aside. Repeat, making 16 paper-thin pancakes. Lay 1 pancake on each of 4 stoneware or other ovenproof plates. Cover with a piece of ham. Place another pancake on top. Cover with a slice of cheese. Repeat this process, ending with cheese. Place the ovenproof plates in a preheated 300° F. oven and bake until cheese melts. Serve at once. Yield: 4 servings.

Microwave Cooking: Place stacked pancakes, ham and cheese on ceramic plates and bake on "high" setting for 1 to 2 minutes.

HAM AND CHEESE WAFFLES

This recipe is good served with applesauce and a sprinkling of cinnamon. Several sausages round out the meal.

★ 1 cup waffle recipe made from commercial mix
½ cup grated Cheddar cheese

½ cup chopped ham
2 tablespoons chopped fresh parsley

Make waffle recipe according to mix instructions. Beat in the cheese. Pour over a preheated waffle iron. Sprinkle with ham and parsley. Bake until steam stops. Yield: 2 servings.

PANCAKES, WAFFLES AND DESSERTS

BANANA PANCAKES WITH PINEAPPLE SAUCE

This is a lovely brunch dish.

★ 1 recipe pancake mix, using 1 cup mix, 1 cup milk, 1 egg and 1 tablespoon butter

2 barely ripe bananas
1½ ounces (3 tablespoons) butter of margarine

Make mix according to package instructions. Cut bananas into ¼-inch slices. Heat butter or margarine in a skillet. Drop batter on hot skillet by the large spoonful. Lay 4 pieces of banana on each pancake. Cook until bubbly on top. Turn and cook for 2 to 3 minutes more. Keep warm in slow oven until all pancakes are baked. Yield: 12 to 14 pancakes, or 4 servings.

Pineapple Sauce

1 cup pineapple juice	1 tablespoon cornstarch
juice of ½ lemon	2 ounces sherry
½ cup sugar	1 tablespoon butter

Place pineapple and lemon juice in a small saucepan. Add sugar and bring to the boil. Mix cornstarch and sherry, and stir into sauce. Cook, stirring, until thickened and clear. Stir in butter. Pour over pancakes. Yield: about 1¼ cups.

BLUEBERRY PANCAKES WITH BLUEBERRY SAUCE

This recipe should be made midsummer when blueberries are at their peak.

★ 1 recipe commercial pancake mix, using 1 cup mix, 1 egg, 1 tablespoon butter	2 ounces (4 tablespoons) butter or margarine
	2 cups blueberries

Make pancakes according to package instructions. Heat skillet and add butter or margarine. Drop batter, by large spoonfuls, on the buttered skillet. Sprinkle 1 tablespoon of blueberries over each pancake. When bubbling on top, flip over and cook for 2 to 3 minutes. Keep warm in a slow oven until all pancakes are cooked. Yield: 12 to 14 pancakes, or 4 servings. Place remaining blueberries in a small saucepan. Add lemon juice, 1 cup water and the sugar. Cook, stirring, for 5 minutes. Mix cornstarch with ¼ cup water. Stir into blueberries. Add butter. Pour over pancakes. Yield: about 2 cups.

Blueberry Sauce

juice of ½ lemon	1 tablespoon cornstarch
1¼ cups of water	1 tablespoon butter
½ cup sugar	

CHOCOLATE WAFFLES

I have suggested whipped cream with these waffles, but ice cream would do just as well.

★ 1 recipe commercial waffles
   from mix, using 2 cups mix,
   2 cups cream, 2 eggs and ⅓
   cup melted butter
6 tablespoons cocoa powder
½ cup sugar

½ cup semisweet chocolate
   bits
1 cup heavy cream
2 tablespoons confectioners'
   sugar
1 teaspoon vanilla extract

Prepare waffle mix according to package instructions, using cream instead of milk. Beat in cocoa and sugar. Heat waffle iron thoroughly. Pour batter on iron. Sprinkle with chocolate bits. Bake until steam stops. Beat cream with sugar and vanilla until stiff. Serve chocolate waffles with a dollop of whipped cream. Yield: 6 servings.

QUICK CHOCOLATE PUDDING

Make this dessert on a busy day when you have no time to fuss.

★ 1½ cups packaged biscuit mix
½ cup granulated sugar
½ cup milk
½ cup brown sugar
1 cup shelled nuts, chopped

ground cinnamon
1½ cups boiling water
6 ounces semisweet chocolate
   morsels
vanilla ice cream

Mix biscuit mix with granulated sugar and milk. Drop in mounds on a greased baking pan 10 x 6 x 1½ inches. Sprinkle with brown sugar, nuts and cinnamon. Pour boiling water over chocolate. Stir until melted. Pour over biscuit mounds. Bake in a preheated 350° F. oven for 35 minutes. Serve in dessert bowls with sauce spooned over top and a dollop of ice cream. Yield: 6 to 8 servings, depending on size of mounds.

QUICK FRUIT SHORTCAKE

Another summertime favorite.

★ 2½ cups commercial biscuit
    mix
¼ cup sugar

2 ounces (4 tablespoons)
    melted margarine
½ cup light cream

Place mix in a bowl. Beat in remaining ingredients. Knead on a floured board to the count of 10. Roll out to a round 1 inch thick. Place in a greased 9-inch cake pan. Bake in a preheated 425° F. oven for 15 to 20 minutes, or until biscuit is puffed and brown on top. Cool, and split into halves.

Fruit Filling

4 cups crushed peaches,
    strawberries, raspberries or
    nectarines
½ cup fine sugar
1 cup heavy cream

3 tablespoons confectioners'
    sugar
1 teaspoon vanilla extract
1 cup sliced peaches or
    nectarines, or whole
    strawberries or raspberries

Mix *crushed* fruit with sugar and allow to stand for 30 minutes at least. Place 2 cups of this fruit over bottom half of shortcake. Cover with the top layer of shortcake and remaining crushed fruit. Whip cream with confectioner's sugar and vanilla until stiff. Spread over top of shortcake. Arrange whole berries or sliced peaches or nectarines over whipped cream. Yield: 8 servings.

Comment: Many fresh fruits such as avocados, nectarines, peaches, pears, apples and apricots discolor when peeled and sliced. This is due to the starch content chemically changing when exposed to air. To prevent this, brush peeled and cut-up fruits with lemon juice.

COUPONS FOR FRUITS AND NUTS

This is my favorite category, because I am a great pear and berry lover. Nothing pleases me more than finding a blackberry patch or a blueberry bog when I am in the country. I wish more parents would give their children fruits and nuts to satisfy their sweet-tooth problems instead of sugared cereals and candies. My boys ate bushels of apples as children and my brother's children consumed boxes of what West Coast denizens call "Japanese oranges."

Fruits and nuts complement every type of food from soups and appetizers to desserts and beverages, but the majority of coupons issued in this category are for dried and canned fruits or for nuts. The recipes, therefore, cover those items. However, I have cheated a little and have included fresh fruits wherever they are pertinent to the recipe. You will find here recipes for appetizers and a soup, one condiment and main-course dishes, and baked goods and desserts.

APPETIZERS AND A SOUP

APPLE-WALNUT APPETIZER

This recipe was concocted by one of my young, ecologically oriented friends. It is a dip to be served with green pepper strips or crackers of your choice.

3 large baking apples,
  unpeeled
1 cup creamed cottage cheese
★ ½ cup finely chopped walnuts

½ teaspoon ground cinnamon
½ teaspoon grated nutmeg
½ teaspoon ground ginger

Place apples in a shallow pan. Add ½ cup water. Prick apples in several places. Bake in a preheated 350° F. oven for 1 hour. Cool, then scrape soft insides from core and skins. Place in a bowl. Beat in remaining ingredients and serve. Yield: approximately 2 cups.

PINEAPPLE-CHEESE BALL

1 pound cream cheese,
  softened
★ 1 can (7 oz.) crushed
  pineapple, well drained
¼ cup minced onion

¼ cup minced green pepper
salt and pepper
2 cups shelled pecans,
  chopped

Mix together well all ingredients except 1 cup pecans. Mold into a ball. Chill thoroughly. Roll in reserved nuts and serve with crackers. Yield: 12 servings.

COLD STRAWBERRY SOUP

This Scandinavian soup tastes like soft ice cream, a little less sweet, however. Serve icy cold, on the patio, as an appetizer during sultry, hot summer days.

★ 2 packages (9 oz. each) frozen
  strawberries
1 cup commercial sour cream

1 tablespoon lemon juice
½ teaspoon ground ginger
dash of grated nutmeg

Purée strawberries in a blender, or force through a sieve. Strain purée to remove seeds. Beat in remaining ingredients. Chill until icy cold. Serve with a dollop of sour cream as garnish. Yield: 6 to 8 servings.

ONE CONDIMENT AND MAIN-COURSE DISHES

APPLE CHUTNEY

When commercial mango chutneys became too expensive, I evolved as good a substitute as possible. Apples being plentiful in the United States, I used them as my base and the result was rewarding. Served with curries, or the chutney chicken following, it makes a truly delectable garnish. Bottled, this chutney keeps indefinitely and makes a wonderful Christmas gift.

2 tablespoons finely chopped
  fresh gingerroot
3 cups vinegar
1 large onion, chopped
4 garlic cloves, crushed
8 large cooking apples, peeled,
  cored and chopped

1 pound brown sugar
1 tablespoon mustard seeds
1 teaspoon salt
1½ teaspoons chili powder
★ 2 cups raisins

Place gingerroot, vinegar, onion, garlic and apples in a large pot. Boil, covered, until apples are soft. Add remaining ingredients and simmer for 15 to 20 minutes. Cool and store in sterilized jars. Yield: 2 quarts.

CHUTNEY CHICKEN

1 ounce (2 tablespoons) butter
  or margarine
2 pounds chicken breasts,
  boned and split
salt and pepper

1 tablespoon lemon juice
1 cup Apple Chutney
  (preceding recipe)
½ cup water

Melt butter or margarine in a skillet. Add chicken breasts and brown on both sides. Salt and pepper to taste. Add lemon juice, chutney and water. Cover and simmer for 15 minutes. Remove chicken and keep warm. Over high heat, reduce pan juices to a glaze. Pour over chicken and serve at once. Yield: 4 servings.

ARMENIAN LAMB

If you live in the southeastern part of the United States, fresh okra is readily available. Steam fresh okra and substitute for frozen okra. This interesting recipe could be accommodated to leftover leg of lamb instead of cubed raw lamb. Add the cooked lamb at the very end, after starting with sautéing of onion and garlic.

2 tablespoons oil	1 teaspoon salt
2 pounds boneless raw lamb, cubed	freshly ground pepper
	1 green pepper, chopped
1 large onion, chopped	★ ½ cup pitted prunes
3 garlic cloves, chopped	★ ½ cup dried apricots
1 can (1 lb.) tomatoes	1½ pounds fresh okra or 2
¼ cup ketchup	packages (10 oz.) frozen

Heat oil in a large skillet. Add lamb and brown on all sides. Drain on paper toweling. Add onion and sauté until limp. Add garlic and sauté for 1 to 2 minutes. Add tomatoes, ketchup, browned meat (if using raw lamb), salt and pepper to taste and simmer for 30 minutes. Add green pepper, prunes and apricots. Cook for 5 minutes. Cook fresh okra in salted water to cover for 20 minutes. Drain. Cook frozen according to package instructions. Stir in okra and, if using leftovers, the lamb. Heat thoroughly. Yield: 6 to 8 servings.

Variation: Use 2 broiling chickens, cut into serving portions in place of the lamb.

DUCK AUX CERISES

Duck à *l'orange* seems to be *de rigueur* in this country. I think cherries are just as good, and the duck is easy to prepare for this recipe.

2 large ducklings, 4 to 5
  pounds each
salt and pepper
★ 1 can or jar (17 oz.) black
  cherries, pitted
juice of 1 lemon

⅓ cup sugar
1 tablespoon grated fresh
  gingerroot
2 ounces Marsala wine
1 tablespoon cornstarch

If ducks are frozen, let them defrost, still wrapped, in the refrigerator for 48 hours. Wash duckling cavities. Salt and pepper inside and out. Prick skins all over with a long-tined fork. Place ducks on a rack in a roasting pan. Roast in preheated 350° F. oven for 1½ hours. Remove from oven. Cool and cut into serving portions (see Comment). Drain cherry juice into a small saucepan. Add lemon juice, sugar and gingerroot, and bring to a boil. Mix Marsala wine with cornstarch. Stir into sauce. As soon as sauce clears and thickens, remove from heat and stir in cherries.

Place duck portions on a rack in a shallow baking dish. Bake in a preheated 350° F. oven for 30 minutes, or until duck is very crisp and dry. Pour heated cherry sauce over duck and serve. Yield: 6 servings.

Comment: Duck always benefits from this precooking, cooling and rebaking system. The cooling process seems to release most of the oil from the duck and the second cooking crisps it beautifully. I prefer cutting each duck into 6 portions. Divide each half into 3 portions. Serve two portions per person.

FRUITED RICE

This Middle Eastern dish is great for vegetarians. The nuts add protein, supplying part of the daily count missed when meat is omitted from the diet.

★ ½ cup pitted prunes, chopped
★ ½ cup dried apricots, chopped
★ ½ cup dried currants
   2 ounces (4 tablespoons)
     butter or margarine

★ ½ cup pignolia nuts, or
   slivered blanched almonds
3 cups processed long-grain
   rice
6 cups water
1 teaspoon salt

Soak prunes, apricots and currants in water to cover for 15 minutes. Drain. Heat butter in a stove-to-oven casserole. Add fruits, nuts and rice and sauté, stirring, for 5 minutes. Add water and salt. Bring to a boil on top of the stove. Cover and bake in a preheated 350° F. oven for 20 minutes, or until all water has been absorbed. Yield: 8 servings.

BAKED GOODS AND DESSERTS

PECAN PIE

One of America's favorite pies.

pastry for 1-crust, 8-inch pie
   (pp. 89 and 93)
★ 1 cup coarsely chopped
   pecans
½ cup granulated sugar
½ cup corn syrup

1 ounce (2 tablespoons)
   melted butter
1½ teaspoons vanilla extract
1 cup heavy cream
2 tablespoons confectioners'
   sugar

Fit pastry into an 8-inch pie dish and crimp the edges. Scatter pecans in the bottom of the pastry. Mix granulated sugar, corn syrup, melted butter and ½ teaspoon vanilla. Pour over pecans. Bake in a preheated 375° F. oven for 45 minutes. Cool. Whip the cream, sweeten with confectioners' sugar and flavor with remaining 1 teaspoon vanilla. Serve with the pie. Yield: 8 servings.

PECAN ROLL

This is an elegant, very rich dessert.

6 eggs, separated
¾ cup granulated sugar
★ 1½ cups grated pecans (see
   Note 1)
1 tablespoon baking powder
flour
2 cups heavy cream

¼ cup confectioners' sugar
1 teaspoon vanilla extract
★ 2 cups canned sliced peaches,
   drained
★ 1 cup canned pitted black
   cherries, well drained

Grease a jellyroll pan. Line it with waxed paper and grease the paper. Set aside. Beat egg yolks until thick and pale-colored. Gradually beat in granulated sugar and beat until very thick and a "ribbon" forms (see Note 2). Fold in pecans. Beat egg whites until soft peaks form. Sprinkle with baking powder and beat until stiff. Carefully fold into egg-yolk mixture. Spread into the prepared jellyroll pan and smooth out. Bake in a preheated 350° F. oven for 20 minutes. Turn out on a floured damp towel. Peel off paper and immediately roll hot cake up in towel from the wide, rather than narrow, side. Refrigerate for 30 minutes.

Whip cream with confectioners' sugar and vanilla until stiff. Unroll cake; discard towel. Spread cake with whipped cream, peaches and cherries. Reroll. Dust with confectioners' sugar and serve. Yield: 10 to 12 servings.

Note 1: Do not grate nuts in a blender. The oil released in the process forms a paste. Use a food processor or nut grater.

Note 2: The "ribbon" forming means that when you lift the beaters above the egg yolks, the batter, as it falls back into the body of the yolks, forms a ribbonlike stream.

CARROT-APPLESAUCE CAKE

Applesauce added to this cake batter makes it moist and succulent.

2¾ cups all-purpose flour
3 teaspoons baking soda
1 teaspoon salt
3 teaspoons ground cinnamon
1 teaspoon grated nutmeg
4 eggs

¾ cup oil
2 cups sugar
1 teaspoon vanilla extract
★ 1 can (1 lb.) applesauce
3 cups shredded carrots
★ 1 cup raisins
★ 1 cup shelled nuts, chopped

Sift flour, baking soda, salt, cinnamon and nutmeg together 3 times, and set aside. Beat eggs. Add oil, sugar and vanilla. Stir in applesauce and carrots. Add dry ingredients, raisins and ½ cup nuts. Heavily grease a 10-inch tube pan or Bundt pan. Pour batter into the pan. Scatter remaining chopped nuts over the top. Bake in a preheated 350° F. oven for 1 hour. Cool on a rack. Serve with a dusting of confectioners' sugar, or with ice cream.

CRANBERRY ICE

¼ cup sugar
1 cup water
½ cup corn syrup
juice of 2 lemons

★ 1 can (1 lb.) cranberry sauce, puréed (see Note)
2 egg whites, beaten stiff
1 cup heavy cream, whipped

Dissolve sugar in water over low heat. Add corn syrup, lemon juice and cranberries. Pour into a bowl and freeze until almost firm. Break up and beat until mushy. Fold in egg whites and heavy cream. Freeze until firm. Yield: 10 to 12 servings.

Note: The best way to purée anything is in a blender. The next best process is to push the product through a sieve with a wooden spoon, or to use a food mill. Scrape puréed food from the outside of the sieve constantly as you proceed. A food processor tends to purée with a gritty, rather than a smooth, consistency.

PUMPKIN TEA BREAD

Tea breads are good to have on hand for breakfast, brunch, snacks or afternoon tea. Make two and freeze one.

3⅓ cups flour
2 teaspoons baking soda
1½ teaspoons salt
½ teaspoon baking powder
1 teaspoon ground cinnamon
1 teaspoon ground cloves

5½ ounces (⅔ cups) margarine
2⅔ cups sugar
4 eggs
★ 1 can (1 lb.) mashed pumpkin
⅔ cup water
★ ⅔ cup shelled nuts, chopped
★ ⅔ cup raisins

Sift flour, baking soda, salt, baking powder, cinnamon and cloves. Grease 2 loaf pans 9 x 5 x 3 inches. Cream margarine and sugar. Beat in eggs, pumpkin and water. Blend in dry ingredients. Stir in nuts and raisins. Spoon into the pans and bake in a preheated 350° F. oven for 1 hour. Yield: 2 loaves.

STRAWBERRY SOUFFLÉ

★ 3 packages (9 oz.) frozen
   strawberries or raspberries
½ cup sugar
1 cup water
4 egg whites, at room
   temperature (see Note, p.
   107)

¼ teaspoon cream of tartar
1⅓ tablespoons cornstarch
Strawberry Sauce (recipe
   follows)

Prepare a 2-quart soufflé dish: coat with butter or margarine; fasten an aluminum foil cuff around the top and coat the inside of the foil with butter or margarine; sprinkle inside of dish and cuff with sugar. Set aside.

Drain the fruit, reserving juices for the sauce. Force berries through a food mill, or purée in a blender (see Note, p. 151). There should be 2 full cups of thick purée. Heat sugar and water, stirring until sugar melts. Boil rapidly over medium-high heat until the syrup registers 238° F. on a candy thermometer. Meanwhile, beat egg whites until stiff. Add cream of tartar. Beating constantly, pour syrup over egg whites. Beat in cornstarch. Fold in purée. Turn into the prepared soufflé dish. Bake in a preheated 375° F. oven for 35 minutes. Serve hot, with strawberry sauce. Yield: 6 to 8 servings.

Strawberry Sauce

1½ cups juice drained from
    frozen berries
pinch of grated nutmeg

½ tablespoon cornstarch, or 1
    teaspoon arrowroot
2 ounces sherry
1 tablespoon butter

If there is not enough juice from berries, add water to make 1½ cups. Pour juice into a saucepan and bring to a boil. Add nutmeg. Dissolve cornstarch or arrowroot in sherry and stir into sauce. Cook until clear and thick. Stir in butter. Yield: 1¾ cups.

ORANGES MEXICAINE

This refreshing, unusual dessert is delicious alone or served over ice cream.

★ 3 cans (11 oz. each) Mandarin
    oranges
2 large oranges, peeled and
    sliced
3 tablespoons lime juice

1½ ounces tequila
1 ounce Cointreau
¼ cup confectioners' sugar
vanilla ice cream

Drain Mandarin oranges. Add to fresh orange slices. Mix lime juice, tequila, Cointreau and confectioners' sugar. Pour over oranges. Marinate for 6 to 8 hours. Serve over ice cream. Yield: 8 servings.

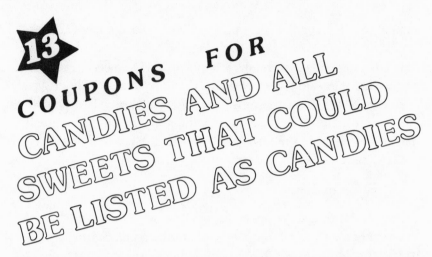

13 COUPONS FOR CANDIES AND ALL SWEETS THAT COULD BE LISTED AS CANDIES

How many recipes can be included in this category? You might be surprised how many things can be done with sweets. I made a cake for my boys when they were young using up all the excess chocolate bars they garnered trickin' and treatin'. The cake was so sweet it made your teeth ache, but it worked. The boys loved it at that tender age, but my husband and I hated it. I did not jot down what I did, needless to say. However, it proved a point: with a little ingenuity, nothing need be wasted.

Hard candies are the easiest to dispose of; just grind them up and add to mousses, custards, etc. Caramel and butterscotch can be incorporated in sauces. Chocolate, unadorned, is the most useful. Gumdrops and jellied candies can be used in baking. I have included a Christmas bread using gumdrops, which is quite unusual and decorative.

Although this chapter is relatively short, the recipes listed are special and I am sure you will enjoy them. Substitute other candies wherever possible, making use of current coupons and house gifts. The only prerequisite is that the alternate be in the same category, i.e., milk chocolate for dark chocolate; hard candy for peppermints; gumdrops for jellied candies; caramels for butterscotch, etc.

One may have a surplus of leftover candies after big holidays like Christmas and Thanksgiving. Rather than let them sit around gathering dust and eventually being discarded, try one of these recipes. Even stock your freezer, if necessary.

BUSY-DAY CHOCOLATE PIE

This is the easiest pie imaginable. It tastes wonderful to all chocolate lovers; very rich, so beware.

½ cup milk
★ 2½ cups miniature
    marshmallows
★ 5 chocolate-almond bars (1.15
    oz. each)

1 cup heavy cream, whipped
1 ounce rum
1 graham-cracker crust (see p.
    114)

Place milk, marshmallows and broken chocolate bars in the top part of a double boiler. Heat over hot water until melted. Beat until smooth. Cool. Fold in whipped cream and rum. Turn into prepared crumb crust. Refrigerate. Yield: 8 servings.

MILK CHOCOLATE FUDGE

Homemade fudge, rather than a commercial box of chocolates, makes a thoughtful house gift.

½ pound (1 cup) butter
4½ cups sugar
★ 1 jar (7 oz.) marshmallow
    creme
1 can (14½ oz.) evaporated
    milk

★ 12 ounces milk chocolate,
    broken up
★ 12 ounces chocolate bits
    2 cups shelled nuts, chopped

Combine butter, sugar, marshmallow creme and evaporated milk in a large heavy-bottomed saucepan. Stir over low heat until sugar has dissolved. Boil over low heat for 7 minutes. Stir occasionally. Off the heat, add chocolates and nuts. Mix well. Pour into a greased pan 9 x 12 x 2 inches. While fudge is still warm, mark lightly with a knife into 1-inch squares. Cool until firm, then cut. Yield: 108 pieces.

CHOCOLATE BOMBE MOUSSE

Prepare this spectacular dessert well ahead and freeze it. Unmold it about 30 minutes before serving, and pour the glaze over it. Your guests will give you a standing ovation.

½ cup sugar
½ cup water
2 egg whites
dash of salt
1½ cups heavy cream,
  whipped

★ ¾ cup grated semisweet
  chocolate
★ ½ cup crushed peppermint
  candies
1 pint chocolate ice cream,
  lightly softened
Cocoa Glaze (recipe follows)

Boil sugar and water until the temperature reaches 230° F. on a candy thermometer (see Comment). Meanwhile beat egg whites with salt until stiff. As soon as syrup reaches 230° F., immediately pour it in a thin stream over egg whites, continuing to beat constantly. Cool completely. Fold in whipped cream, chocolate and peppermint candy. Line an 8-cup mold with the ice cream. Fill the cavity with the mousse. Place in the freezer. Unmold by placing a cloth wrung out in almost boiling hot water over the bottom. Mold will release onto a serving plate. Garnish with the glaze, below. Yield: 8 to 10 servings.

Comment: A candy thermometer is a valuable adjunct to your kitchen equipment. It takes the guesswork out of testing syrups for confections. If you do not have one, test syrup by drizzling a tiny amount into a glass of cold water. If the syrup forms a ball that is soft and malleable to the touch, it is at the "soft ball" stage, or about 230° to 244° F. If the ball of syrup is hard to the touch, or at the "hard ball" stage, it is about 245° to 255° F. You must test constantly while the syrup is boiling. When it appears to "string" or form a long cobwebby thread when you lift the spoon above the pot and allow the syrup to drip into the saucepan, it is usually ready to start testing for the "soft ball" stage. The longer it cooks, the harder the ball.

Cocoa Glaze

⅓ cup heavy cream
1½ ounces (3 tablespoons)
   butter or margarine

½ cup cocoa powder
¾ cup sugar
½ teaspoon vanilla extract

Place first 4 ingredients in a small saucepan and cook for 4 minutes. Add vanilla. Cool. Yield: 1 cup.

CHRISTMAS CARROT TEA BREAD

This tea bread was evolved to compete with all those breakfast breads served during the holiday season. I think it is particularly American.

★ 1 cup red and green
   gumdrops, finely chopped
   (see Note)
1½ cups all-purpose flour
½ teaspoon salt
½ teaspoon baking soda
¼ teaspoon baking powder
1 teaspoon ground cinnamon

½ cup chopped nuts
½ cup raisins
2 eggs
¾ cup sugar
½ cup oil
½ teaspoon vanilla extract
1 cup shredded raw carrots

Coat gumdrops evenly with 2 tablespoons of flour. Sift remaining flour with salt, baking soda, baking powder and cinnamon. Add nuts and raisins and toss well. Beat eggs, sugar and oil in another bowl. Add vanilla. Stir in flour mixture. Add carrots and gumdrops. Spoon into a well-greased loaf pan 9 x 5 x 3 inches. Bake in a preheated 350° F. oven for 1 hour. Cool on a rack and serve.

Note: Chopping gumdrops is difficult. They are so sticky they cling to the knife. This problem is easily combatted by keeping a glass of water nearby and dipping the knife into it constantly to keep the blade wet.

CREAM PUFFS WITH CARAMEL SAUCE

Pâte à chou is the paste used to make cream puffs. The secret is to beat in whole eggs while the dough is hot. This is easier to do in an electric mixer. As soon as the flour mixture leaves the sides of the pan (see recipe), quickly turn it into the warmed bowl of your electric mixer and proceed. The bowl must be warmed to keep the paste from cooling before eggs are beaten in.

Pâte à Chou

1 cup water
¼ pound (½ cup) butter
¼ teaspoon salt

1 cup sifted flour (see Note)
4 eggs

Boil water, butter and salt. Add flour all at once and beat, over low heat, until dough leaves the sides of pan. Remove from heat and immediately beat in eggs, one at a time, beating vigorously after each addition. Mixture should be smooth and glossy. Drop by the tablespoon on a greased cookie sheet. Bake in a preheated 450° F. oven for 15 minutes. Reduce heat to 350° F. and bake for a further 30 to 35 minutes. Remove from oven. Cut off the top quarter of each puff and scrape out gummy uncooked center. Return puffs to the turned-off oven with door open to dry out.

Fill with *Crème Pâtissière* and drizzle with caramel sauce. Yield: 10 large puffs.

Note: To sift and measure flour at the same time, place a flat-topped measuring cup on a sheet of waxed paper. Sift flour over the cup until it is filled. Using a knife, smooth the top off level with the rim. Return to the flour bin any flour left on the waxed paper.

Crème Pâtissière

½ cup sugar
5 egg yolks
⅔ cup flour
2 cups milk, scalded

1 tablespoon butter
1½ teaspoons vanilla extract
or 1½ ounces rum

Place sugar and egg yolks in a heavy-bottomed saucepan. Beat well. Beat in flour. Slowly beat in scalded milk. Cook over low heat, stirring constantly, until mixture thickens. Beat vigorously to remove lumps. Beat in butter and vanilla or rum. Cool, then use to fill puffs. Yield: approximately 2 cups.

Note: *Crème pâtissière* is rather difficult to make. The egg yolks and milk have a tendency to scorch quickly if you do not stir vigorously over very low heat. If you are nervous about doing this, you could fill your puffs with whipped and sweetened heavy cream. Many people prefer this to the custard.

Caramel Sauce

★ 30 caramels
½ cup water
1 tablespoon rum

Place caramels and water in a saucepan. Cook, stirring, until caramels are melted and smooth. Beat in rum. Yield: 1½ cups.

MOCK PRALINE PIE

Praline is a confection made from caramelized sugar that is poured over pecans, or other nuts, allowed to harden, then pulverized in a blender. Before pulverizing, it is really a hard toffee, so why not make it from commercial toffee? That is why I call it "mock" praline.

¾ teaspoon unflavored gelatin
1½ tablespoons cold water
¼ cup sugar
½ cup prepared very strong coffee, preferably espresso
15 ounces ricotta cheese
1 tablespoon rum, or 1 teaspoon vanilla extract

1 cup heavy cream, whipped
1 tablespoon confectioners' sugar
½ teaspoon vanilla extract
★ 1 package (6 oz.) butterscotch toffee, crushed
1 teaspoon ground cinnamon
1 cracker-crumb crust (p. 114)

Soften gelatin in cold water. Dissolve sugar in coffee over low heat, stirring constantly. Add gelatin and stir until dissolved. Cool. Beat cheese well. Add coffee mixture. Stir in rum. Fold in half of the whipped cream. Stir confectioners' sugar and ½ teaspoon vanilla into remaining whipped cream. Mix crushed toffee and cinnamon and set aside. Pour filling into cracker-crumb pie shell. Garnish with remaining whipped cream. Chill. Just before serving sprinkle with toffee-cinnamon mixture. Yield: 8 to 10 servings.

CRUSHED CANDY PUDDING

Serve this cakelike pudding warm with ice cream. I used to make it for my boys after Halloween to use some of the many hard candies they acquired.

1 cup brown sugar
2 cups flour
¼ pound (½ cup) margarine
1 egg
1 cup buttermilk or soured milk

1 teaspoon baking soda
dash salt
1 teaspoon vanilla
½ cup shelled nuts, chopped
★ 1 cup crushed hard candies

Combine sugar and flour. Cut in margarine. Reserve ⅔ cup of this mixture. Beat egg, buttermilk, baking soda, salt and vanilla into the larger portion of flour mixture. Spoon into a greased pan 9 x 12 x 2 inches. Top with reserved flour mixture, the chopped nuts and crushed candies. Bake in a preheated 350° F. oven for 30 minutes. Yield: 8 servings.

POPCORN BALLS

Another Christmas favorite in our household. We used to make these popcorn balls, string them on a cord and decorate the tree. Tiny hands loved to pry gooey pieces of popcorn from the balls when no one was looking.

1½ cups maple syrup (see Note)
1 tablespoon butter
3 tablespoons water

1 teaspoon vanilla extract
★ 3 quarts popcorn (do it yourself, use Cracker Jack or buy commercial popcorn)

Heat maple syrup, butter and water in a large saucepan and cook until syrup reaches 252° F. on a candy thermometer. Remove from heat and stir in vanilla and popcorn. Form into 2-inch balls. If you want to hang them, string a large darning needle with cord. Run cord through the center of each ball; tie a large knot or place a wooden bead between the balls to keep them apart.

Note: Maple syrup is expensive and hard to obtain in many parts of the country. Regular corn syrup and pancake syrups may be substituted. I have noticed many coupons issued for syrups. Take advantage of one of these when planning to have a popcorn-making session.

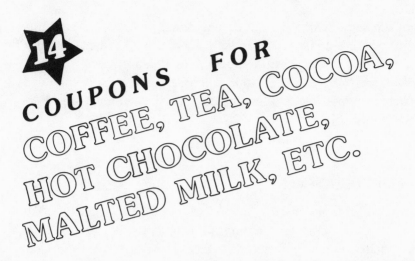

COUPONS FOR COFFEE, TEA, COCOA, HOT CHOCOLATE, MALTED MILK, ETC.

Coffee coupons appear regularly in magazines and newspapers. They usually fall into the instant and freeze-dried categories, both regular and decaffeinated, but many firms issue coupons toward the purchase of 1-pound cans of freshly ground coffee. Tea and cocoa coupons are not quite so common. I have lumped the three together along with hot chocolates, malted milks and any other nourishing hot drinks that are likely to be introduced.

Mocha is a delightful and popular flavor often used in baking. The easiest way to make it is to combine cocoa and instant coffee. Leftover breakfast coffee can be used in baking and sauces or can be refrigerated for iced coffee. Leftover tea should be poured off the tea leaves and stored in a glass or plastic container. It can be used for punches, desserts or iced tea.

Beverage coupons can be used more in making desserts than other dishes, but I have included some interesting main dishes as well. Some are traditional recipes which I have prepared many times both as a restaurateur and hostess; some are innovations. All taste great!

MAIN-COURSE DISHES

A dagger following a recipe title indicates that the recipe was given to me by the Tea Council of the USA, Inc. I have adjusted a few to my own taste, but they are essentially as they were given to me and are excellent. My thanks goes to this organization for its cooperation.

COFFEE-GLAZED HAM

1 cup honey
★ ½ cup prepared very strong
  coffee
1 teaspoon ground allspice
6 to 8 pounds uncooked ham
  with rind

whole cloves
dried apricots or canned
  pineapple rings
maraschino cherries

Mix honey, coffee and allspice in a small pot. Cook over very low heat, stirring occasionally, for 15 minutes. Cool. Place ham on a rack in a shallow pan. Cover. Bake in a preheated 300° F. oven for 25 minutes per pound. At 1 hour before baking time is completed, remove ham from oven, remove rind, and score the fat in a criss-cross pattern, forming diamonds about 1½ inches in size. Using whole cloves and toothpicks, skewer an apricot or pineapple slice in each diamond. With a toothpick, skewer a cherry in the center of each piece of fruit. Return ham to oven. During the last hour of baking, baste the ham generously with coffee glaze every 15 minutes. Allow ham to rest for 15 minutes before carving. Yield: 14 to 16 servings.

Microwave Cooking: Place ham in oven, cover with waxed paper and bake on "medium" setting for 12 to 15 minutes per pound. Remove ham from oven, cut off rind, score and proceed with recipe. Cook on "high" setting for 5 minutes.

APRICOT-TEA HAM GLAZE †

This is one of my Tea Council recipes, another delicious and unusual ham glaze.

Blend 1 tablespoon instant tea powder and 1 tablespoon lemon juice into 12 ounces apricot jam. Cook ham according to directions on the label. About 30 minutes before the ham is done, score fat in any pattern that suits your fancy and brush well with glaze mixture. Continue baking for 15 minutes, then brush again with glaze. This glaze is also delicious with duckling or a roast of pork.

Microwave Cooking: Follow same procedure used for Coffee-Glazed Ham (preceding recipe).

RED-EYE BREAKFAST

This is a traditional Southern breakfast; use a large slice of smoked Virginia or country-cured ham.

1-pound slice of smoked
   Virginia or country-cured ham
★ 2 cups freshly brewed coffee

1 dozen eggs
6 English muffins, split and
   toasted

Trim ham slice of excess fat. Place fat in a large skillet and render it (see Comment) over low heat. Add ham slice and brown on both sides over fairly high heat. Add coffee, cover and simmer for 3 to 4 minutes. Remove ham and keep warm. Reduce heat; liquid should be barely boiling. Break eggs into coffee-ham gravy. Cover and simmer for 3 to 5 minutes, or until whites are firm and yolks are still soft. Meanwhile, toast muffins and arrange 2 halves on each of 6 serving plates. Top each muffin with a small piece of ham. Top with a poached egg, pour a spoonful of the "red-eye" gravy over top, and serve. Yield: 6 servings.

Note: You may prefer the "red-eye" gravy thickened. To do so, follow instructions for "sauce-making" (Comment, p. 92), using ingredients for a medium-thick sauce and the "red-eye" liquid for the sauce base. While making the sauce, keep eggs and muffins warm in a 175° F. oven.

Comment: Rendering means to place fat over very low heat and cook, uncovered, until fat is released from the tissues.

APRICOT-BROILED SWORDFISH

This is an unusual and delicious way to serve swordfish.

1 can (12 oz.) apricot nectar
★ ½ cup prepared very strong coffee
¼ cup dry white wine
1 tablespoon oil
1 tablespoon butter

2 pounds swordfish steaks
salt and freshly ground pepper
paprika
1 can (1 lb.) apricots, well drained

Mix apricot nectar, coffee and wine. Heat to boiling and cook uncovered for 5 minutes. Heat oil and butter until butter melts. Brush swordfish steaks with butter mixture, and sprinkle with salt, pepper and paprika to taste. Broil for 5 minutes. Turn. Pour half of the coffee mixture over the fish steaks. Broil for another 5 minutes. Heat apricots in remaining sauce. Spoon sauce and apricots over the fish. Serve at once. Yield: 4 servings.

Microwave Cooking: Place prepared steaks in microwave oven and cook on "high" setting for 4 minutes. Brush with sauce and cook for another 3 to 4 minutes. Heat sauce and apricots in a glass, plastic or ceramic dish, covered with wax paper on "high" setting for 1 minute just before serving.

COFFEE-ROASTED LEG OF LAMB

This is an expensive dish, but well worth the cost. Lamb should not be overcooked. It shouldn't be as rare as beef, but pink in the middle; cooking time makes the difference between dull lamb and great lamb. The coffee adds an attractive piquancy.

leg of lamb, 5 to 6 pounds
1 garlic clove
2 tablespoons soy sauce
1 tablespoon oil
2 carrots, scraped and cut into
  2-inch chunks
2 celery ribs, chopped

1 cup chicken broth
★ 1 cup prepared strong coffee
½ cup heavy cream
2 teaspoons honey
1 tablespoon snipped fresh
  dill, or 1 teaspoon dried
beurre manié (p. 69)

Remove the "fell" of the lamb (the heavy outer membrane) with a large sharp knife, or ask butcher to do it for you. Discard fell. Cut off most of the fat, leaving small patches. Sliver the garlic clove. Pierce surface of lamb at intervals with a sharp knife and force slivers of garlic into the slashes. Brush leg of lamb with soy sauce, then with oil. Roast the lamb in a preheated 450° F. oven for 15 minutes. Reduce heat to 350° F. Place carrots and celery around meat. Roast for 30 minutes. Add broth and cook for 15 minutes. Mix coffee, cream and honey, and pour over lamb. Roast for 45 minutes. Remove lamb from oven to a heated platter. Pour juices from meat into a saucepan. Skim off (see Note) as much fat as possible. Add the dill to the juices. Bring sauce to a boil. Beat in as much *beurre manié* as needed to attain desired thickness. Serve sauce with lamb. Yield: 12 servings.

Note: A good way to remove excess fat from a hot liquid (degreasing) is to blot it up with paper toweling. The fat is absorbed by the paper, leaving the liquid free.

Microwave Cooking: Prepare lamb as in the recipe, and cover with waxed paper. Bake at "medium" setting for 9 to 11 minutes per pound, pouring liquid over meat after first 20 minutes of cooking.

PORK ROAST WITH COFFEE SAUCE

The flavor of coffee lends itself particularly well to pork.

4 pounds boneless loin of pork, trimmed of most of its fat
freshly ground pepper and salt
1 garlic clove
several strips of orange rind zest (see Note)
1 onion, minced

2 tomatoes, peeled, seeded and chopped
2 tablespoons chopped fresh parsley
½ teaspoon sugar
★ ¾ cup prepared strong coffee
1 tablespoon lemon juice
juice of 1 orange

Sprinkle pork with pepper and salt. Pierce surface at intervals with a sharp knife. Sliver the garlic clove and orange rind. Force garlic and orange-rind slivers into the holes in the pork. Place pork on a rack in a shallow baking pan. Bake in a preheated 300° F. oven for 40 minutes per pound. Remove from pan and keep warm on a heated platter or carving board.

Pour 2 tablespoons of pork fat into a saucepan. Add onion and sauté until limp. Scrape crusty drippings from roasting pan and add to saucepan, along with tomatoes, parsley, sugar, ½ teaspoon salt and pepper to taste. Simmer for 10 minutes, or until tomatoes are mushy. Add coffee, lemon and orange juices. Cook over high heat for 5 minutes to reduce liquid slightly. Serve with sliced pork. Yield: 8 servings.

Note: The "zest" of the orange is the very thin orange-colored outer skin or rind. The inner white part, the "pith" can cause a bitter taste in dishes.

Microwave Cooking: Prepare roast as described, cover with waxed paper, and bake at "medium" setting for 13 to 15 minutes per pound.

COFFEE-BARBECUED SPARERIBS

This is a variation on sweet-and-sour spareribs. You'll find it a tasty innovation.

5 to 6 pounds lean spareribs
salt and pepper
★ 1 cup prepared strong coffee
½ cup molasses
¼ cup prepared mustard

1 tablespoon Worcestershire
  sauce
½ cup cider vinegar
dash of Tabasco

Sprinkle spareribs with salt and pepper and place them in a shallow baking dish. Bake in a preheated 325° F. oven for 1½ hours. Pour off all grease. Cool meat and cut into individual ribs. Mix all remaining ingredients, heat and stir until well blended. Pour a small amount into a baking dish. Place spareribs on top of sauce. Brush half of remaining sauce over the ribs. Return to the oven and bake, brushing with sauce every 15 minutes, for 1 hour. Yield: 4 to 6 servings.

Microwave Cooking: Precook the spareribs at "medium" setting for 45 minutes. Pour off grease, cut into individual ribs. Continue with recipe. Bake at "high" setting for 10 minutes. Brush with sauce every 8 to 10 minutes during last cooking period.

BAKED GOODS AND DESSERTS

SWEDISH BREAD

This is called "limpa" bread by some and is particularly good.

1 cup milk
¼ cup honey
1 tablespoon butter
★ 1 heaping teaspoon instant
   coffee powder
1 teaspoon fennel seeds
2 teaspoons salt
grated rind of 1 orange
3 tablespoons sugar

1 envelope active dry yeast
¼ cup lukewarm water (105°
   to 115° F.)
½ teaspoon ground cloves
1 cup rye flour
3 cups white flour
1 egg white, beaten with 1
   tablespoon water

Scald milk. Place honey, butter, coffee powder, fennel seeds and salt in a large bowl. Add milk, orange rind and sugar. Stir to mix well, then cool to tepid. Dissolve yeast in lukewarm water. Stir into milk mixture. Add cloves and rye flour and 1½ cups white flour; mix well. Stir in remaining flour. Turn dough out on a floured board and knead for 8 to 10 minutes, or until smooth and elastic. Place in a greased bowl, turn once to grease top, and cover with plastic wrap. Allow dough to rise until doubled in bulk (see Comment, p. 22).

Punch down, and shape into 2 round balls. Slash a shallow cross in the top of each ball. Place dough balls on a greased cookie sheet and allow to rise again until doubled in bulk. Brush with the egg-white mixture. Bake in a preheated 350° F. oven for 25 minutes. Yield: 2 loaves.

ORANGE TEA MUFFINS †

Tea adds an unusual quality to these muffins.

2 eggs
1 cup milk
★ ½ teaspoon instant tea powder
¼ cup cooking oil
1 teaspoon grated orange rind

2 cups sifted all-purpose flour
¼ cup sugar
3 teaspoons double-acting
    baking powder
1 teaspoon salt

Oil the bottoms only of twelve 2½-inch muffin cups; set aside. Beat eggs lightly; stir in milk, tea, oil and orange rind. Sift together flour, sugar, baking powder and salt. Add dry ingredients to first mixture all at once and stir until flour is just moistened. Do not overmix; batter should be lumpy. Pour into the prepared muffin cups. Bake in preheated 400° F. oven for about 25 minutes, or until muffins are golden and slightly shrinking from sides. Run a small spatula around sides and flip sideways to prevent sogginess while keeping warm; or remove and place in cloth-lined muffin warmer. Serve with sweet butter and strawberry jam. Yield: 12 muffins.

TEA-LICIOUS PIE †

A pie for all those tea lovers in America.

1½ cups plus 6 tablespoons
    sugar
⅓ cup cornstarch
★ 2 tablespoons instant tea
    powder
1¾ cups water

3 eggs, separated
1½ ounces (3 tablespoons)
    butter
1 baked 9-inch pastry shell
¼ teaspoon cream of tartar

Mix 1½ cups sugar and the cornstarch in a saucepan; dissolve instant tea in 1¾ cups water and stir into sugar mixture. Place over medium heat and cook, stirring constantly, until mixture thickens and boils. Boil, still stirring, for 1 minute longer. Beat the egg yolks. Slowly stir half of the hot mixture into beaten egg yolks, then blend with remaining hot mixture in saucepan. Continue cooking over very low heat, stirring constantly, for 1 minute longer. Remove from heat and blend in butter. Turn into the pie shell. Beat egg whites and cream of tartar until frothy. Beat in remaining 6 tablespoons sugar gradually; continue beating until meringue is very stiff and glossy. Pile meringue on filling, arranging in swirls that touch edges of pastry (see Note). Bake in a preheated 350° F. oven for about 15 minutes, or until top is golden brown. Cool in a slightly warm spot away from drafts. Yield: 6 to 8 servings.

Note: Meringue has a way of sliding around on cornstarch-based pie fillings. Sealing it to the edges of the pastry prevents this.

CHOCOLATE LIQUEUR CAKE

This cake is quick, easy and foolproof.

1 box (18½ oz.) chocolate cake mix	★ ½ cup prepared very strong coffee
1 package (3¾ oz.) instant chocolate pudding	4 ounces Kahlúa
4 eggs	1 ounce anise liqueur or brandy
½ cup cooking oil	Liqueur Glaze (recipe follows)

Combine cake mix and dry pudding. Add eggs, one at a time, beating well after each addition. Beat in oil, coffee, Kahlúa and other liqueur. Beat until very well mixed. Pour into a well-greased and floured 10-inch Bundt pan. Bake in a preheated 350° F. oven for 45 to 50 minutes. Turn out onto a rack. While cake is still warm, pour liqueur glaze over top of cake. Yield: 10 to 12 servings.

Liqueur Glaze

1 cup confectioners' sugar	1 tablespoon Kahlúa
1 tablespoon prepared coffee	1 teaspoon anise liqueur or brandy

Mix well and pour over warm cake.

BÛCHE DE NOËL

This is a traditional French Christmas cake. I have served it for as long as I can remember. It always creates a sensation and tastes wonderful.

4 eggs, separated
¼ cup sugar
pinch of salt
¼ cup sifted flour
¼ cup sifted cornstarch
★ ½ cup sifted cocoa powder,
  plus extra for finishing

1 teaspoon vanilla extract
Mocha Buttercream (recipe
  follows)
green pistachio nuts
small sprig of holly

Grease a jellyroll pan, line with waxed paper and grease the paper. Sprinkle with flour, and swirl around to distribute evenly. Tap out excess flour. Beat egg whites until soft peaks form. Gradually beat in sugar and salt. Beat until very stiff, but not dry. Sift flour, cornstarch and cocoa. Beat egg yolks lightly. Add vanilla to yolks. Stir a large spoonful of whites into yolks. Pour this over remaining egg whites and fold together carefully. Sprinkle dry ingredients over top and fold together. Spread evenly in prepared pan. Bake in a preheated 350° F. oven for 12 minutes. Cover with a damp, cocoa-sprinkled dish towel. Quickly invert the cake on the towel. Remove pan and peel off waxed paper. Roll cake up, from a long side, in the damp towel. Refrigerate.

When cake is cooled, unroll and spread with some of the mocha buttercream. Roll up, place on a long board, and spread with remaining buttercream. Run the tines of a fork lengthwise over the entire surface of the cake. Pat pistachio nuts over each end. Decorate center top with holly. Voilà! a Christmas log or *bûche de Noël.* Yield: 10 servings.

MOCHA BUTTERCREAM

Traditional buttercream is not easy to make, but it tastes delicious. You need a candy thermometer to cook the syrup to the exact temperature required. This buttercream is very rich, so do not spread too thick a layer on your cake.

¾ cup sugar
½ cup water
5 egg yolks

6 ounces chocolate morsels
★ ¼ cup prepared strong coffee
6 ounces (¾ cup) sweet butter
1 ounce brandy

Place sugar and water in a small saucepan. Heat to boiling, stirring until sugar is dissolved. Place a candy thermometer in the syrup and boil rapidly without stirring until thermometer registers 235° F. Meanwhile, beat egg yolks until very thick and pale and a "ribbon" forms (see Note, p. 150). Pour prepared hot syrup over beaten yolks in a thin stream, beating constantly as you pour. Continue to beat until the mixture cools. Place in refrigerator until chilled. Melt chocolate in the coffee over hot water. Cool. Cream butter well. Beat cold egg-yolk mixture into butter bit by bit. Beat in coffee-chocolate mixture and the brandy. Yield: enough buttercream for a large cake.

COCOA SOUR-MILK CAKE

I tried for years to develop a really good, dark chocolate cake that would use milk or cream that had soured. This good chocolate cake is the result. Naturally, it tastes richer with soured cream, but it tastes good either way. This large 3-layer cake is wonderful for children's birthday parties.

2½ cups all-purpose flour
2 teaspoons baking soda
★ 1 cup cocoa powder
½ teaspoon salt
½ pound (1 cup) margarine

2 cups sugar
4 eggs
1 cup soured milk or cream
 (see Note)
1 teaspoon vanilla extract
1 cup boiling water

Sift flour, baking soda, cocoa and salt together 3 times. Cream margarine and sugar until light and fluffy. Add eggs one at a time. Add flour mixture and soured milk or cream, alternately (see Note, p. 175). Add vanilla and boiling water. Line 3 well-greased -inch pans with waxed paper, then grease the paper. Spoon cake into the pans. Bake in a preheated 375° F. oven for 40 minutes. Cool on racks and spread with 1½ recipes of Chocolate Frosting (p. 98) (see Comment). Yield: 12 to 14 servings.

Note: If a recipe calls for soured cream or milk and you have none, add 1 tablespoon lemon juice or vinegar to 1 cup milk and allow it to sit several hours. Buttermilk may be substituted if you prefer.

Comment: To ice a cake, cut four strips of waxed paper and arrange around the edges of a serving plate. Place a layer over the strips. Completely frost the layer. Place another layer on top, lining it up so that the cake is even if your oven produces a lopsided result (this is usually due to uneven temperature in the oven). Ice the final layer. If a three tier cake, repeat. Gently pull waxed paper strips from under the cake to remove drippings.

CHOCOLATE SWEET-POTATO CAKE

The addition of grated raw vegetables to cakes and tea breads gives them a moist, delicious texture. I often make the following recipe during winter months when sweet potatoes are plentiful.

2½ cups flour
★ ½ cup cocoa powder
2½ teaspoons baking powder
1½ teaspoons baking soda
1 teaspoon salt
2 cups sugar

6 ounces (¾ cup) margarine
3 eggs
1 teaspoon vanilla extract
¾ cup milk
2 cups shredded raw sweet
   potatoes
1 cup chopped nuts

Sift flour, cocoa, baking powder, baking soda and salt. Cream sugar with margarine until fluffy. Add eggs one at a time, beating well after each addition. Beat in vanilla. Add flour mixture alternately with milk (see Note). Stir in sweet potatoes and nuts. Turn into a well-greased 10-inch Bundt pan. Bake in a preheated 350° F. oven for 1 hour. Cool on a rack. Serve with a dusting of confectioners' sugar or frosting of your choice (see Index for pages). Yield: 10 to 12 servings.

Note: When a recipe uses the term "alternately," stir in one quarter of the dry ingredients and one quarter of the wet. Repeat until all is used.

RUM-COFFEE CREAM CAKE

As a restaurateur I served this cake many times. People were always pleasantly surprised by the rummy-coffee taste.

1¼ cups flour
1¼ teaspoons baking powder
pinch of salt
6 ounces (¾ cup) butter or
  margarine
¾ cup plus 3 tablespoons
  granulated sugar
3 eggs

★ 2 cups prepared strong black
  coffee
4 ounces rum
1 cup heavy cream
3 tablespoons confectioners'
  sugar
1 teaspoon vanilla extract
½ cup sliced blanched
  almonds

Sift flour, baking powder and salt. Cream butter or margarine with ¾ cup granulated sugar until light and fluffy. Beat in eggs one at a time. Fold in flour mixture. Turn into a well-greased 1½-quart ring mold. Bake in a preheated 375° F. oven for 25 minutes. Remove from ring mold and cool on a rack.

Return cake to ring mold. Pierce cake all over with a metal skewer. Place coffee in a saucepan. Add 3 tablespoons granulated sugar and stir over medium heat until sugar melts; remove from heat and cool. Add rum, and pour syrup over pierced cake. Allow cake to absorb completely the coffee-rum mixture. Turn out onto a decorative cake plate. Beat heavy cream with confectioners' sugar until soft peaks form. Beat in vanilla. Completely cover cake with whipped cream. Sprinkle with sliced almonds. Chill before serving. Yield: 8 to 10 servings.

CHOCOLATE CRÊPES

Crêpes are lovely to serve on special occasions. Don't be afraid of them. Read my Comment and the recipe carefully and you'll have no problem.

2 eggs	★ 2 tablespoons cocoa powder
¼ cup sugar	1 tablespoon melted butter
1 cup light cream	1 teaspoon vanilla
½ cup flour	

Place all ingredients in the container of a blender or food processor and blend; scrape down the sides and blend again. Allow batter to rest for 2 hours before making crêpes.

If you do not have a blender: beat eggs; add sugar and cream and beat well. Beat in flour, cocoa, butter and vanilla. Allow batter to rest for 2 hours.

Brush a hot 6-inch crêpe pan with melted butter. Spoon 1 large tablespoon of batter onto the pan. Quickly swirl it around to coat bottom of crêpe pan evenly. Cook over medium heat until crêpe has "set." Turn over onto an adjacent, greased hot frying pan to "set" on the other side. Repeat until all batter is used. Yield: 16 crêpes, approximately.

Fill crêpes with sweetened whipped cream, ice cream or Chocolate Mousse (p. 119), roll and dust with confectioners' sugar.

Comment: A crêpe pan should be hidden away and kept for crêpes only. It takes time to season a good crêpe pan and using it for other purposes spoils the surface.

All crêpe batters should rest for several hours, or overnight, to allow the flour to absorb the liquid completely before cooking.

When storing crêpes, separate them for cooling, so they do not stick together. When cooled, stack them without placing waxed paper between the crêpes; this way they keep each other moist and hence are easier to roll before serving.

IRISH-WHISKEY COFFEE PIE

Don't serve this sophisticated pie to your teetotaler friends or your little children.

1 envelope unflavored gelatin
4 ounces Irish whiskey
★ 1 tablespoon instant coffee
   powder
3 egg yolks
½ cup sugar
dash of salt

2 cups heavy cream
1 Cereal Crumb Crust (p. 38)
2 tablespoons confectioners'
   sugar
1 teaspoon vanilla extract
1 ounce semisweet chocolate,
   shaved (see p. 107)

Sprinkle gelatin over whiskey. Place over hot water and stir until gelatin is dissolved. Add coffee. Cool to a syrupy consistency. Beat yolks with sugar and salt until very thick and lemon-colored. Stir in gelatin mixture. Whip 1 cup of the cream, and fold into the gelatin mixture. Turn into the prepared crumb crust. Chill until set. Whip the second cup of cream, sweeten it with confectioners' sugar and flavor with vanilla. Spread on top of the pie. Sprinkle with shaved chocolate. Yield: 8 servings.

TEA-SPICED PRUNES †

Rinse 1 pound tenderized prunes. Put in a saucepan with 1 sliced seedless orange, 1 sliced lemon, and a stick of cinnamon. Add enough cold water to cover prunes. Bring to a boil and simmer gently for 10 minutes. Remove from heat and stir in 1 tablespoon instant tea. Cover tightly and let stand in refrigerator at least overnight. Prunes will be plump and tender, but not too soft, and will have an intriguing new flavor.

You might try this recipe using apricots in place of prunes.

JOHN'S COFFEE LIQUEUR

I found this recipe tacked up on my Canadian brother's kitchen wall. It is the best coffee liqueur I have ever tasted.

★ 8 heaping teaspoons instant coffee powder
3½ cups sugar

1 quart water
2½ cups vodka
3 teaspoons vanilla extract

Bring the first 3 ingredients to a full boil. Simmer, uncovered, for 1 hour. Cool. Add vodka and vanilla. Bottle and allow to rest for at least 30 days. Yield: 2 quarts.

COUPONS FOR SODAS, JUICES AND DRINKS

Skimming through my coupon collection I find I have coupons for lemonade, grape and orange juices, Perrier Mineral Water, tomato juice, ginger ale, frozen concentrates, etc. I even have one for beer, which I don't drink. However I do cook with all these liquids and the recipes following illustrate some of the interesting uses to which they can be put, in main-course dishes and vegetables, as well as baked goods and one drink.

I enjoy cooking in a variety of liquids. If you are dieting, liquids can add unusual taste qualities to a food product without adding much in the way of calories. Ginger ale, for instance, is a good poaching liquid, and unsweetened fruit juices do wonders for vegetables. A small amount of frozen juice concentrate added to a sauce makes an instant sweet-and-sour effect.

ONE APPETIZER, MAIN-COURSE DISHES AND VEGETABLES

COCKTAIL MEATBALLS

This is an easy, unusual way to serve meatballs, while making use of some of your ginger ale coupons.

2 pounds beef chuck, ground
2 eggs
2 cups bread crumbs
1 small onion, grated
1 teaspoon garlic powder

1 teaspoon salt
freshly ground pepper
3 tablespoons oil
1 bottle (12 oz.) chili sauce
★ 8 ounces ginger ale

Mix beef, eggs, bread crumbs, onion, garlic powder, salt and pepper to taste. Form in 1-inch balls. Heat oil in a skillet. Brown meatballs, shaking pan often to maintain round shape of balls. Drain on paper toweling. Mix chili sauce and ginger ale in a 3-quart casserole. Heat to boiling. Add meatballs. Simmer covered for 20 minutes, or until done. Yield: approximately 48 meatballs.

BUTTERFLIED LEG OF LAMB

Start this the day before you plan to serve it. The lamb can be broiled or cooked on an open grill. Since it is opened flat, it needs only about 30 minutes on the grill for a pink middle. Slice slightly on the diagonal when cutting.

boned and butterflied leg of
  lamb, 6 pounds
½ cup honey
★ ½ cup apple juice

4 or 5 garlic cloves, crushed
¾ cup soy sauce
4 ounces dry white wine
1 tablespoon cornstarch

Have your butcher butterfly the lamb; it will be spread out flat, rather than being rolled and tied. Remove fell, or have your butcher do it, and trim off all fat. Mix honey and apple juice. Bring to a boil and stir until honey has dissolved. Add garlic and soy sauce. Pour over lamb and marinate overnight. Turn as often as possible.

Drain lamb and place on a rack in a shallow roasting pan. Pour ¾ cup marinade and ¾ cup water in bottom of pan. Roast in a preheated 300° F. oven for 1½ to 2 hours. Remove from oven and allow to rest for 10 minutes before carving.

Meanwhile, pour juices from the roasting pan into a saucepan. Add wine and all but ¼ cup of remaining marinade. Dissolve cornstarch in ¼ cup marinade. Bring sauce to boil, stir in cornstarch, and cook until thickened. Pour over sliced meat. Yield: 8 to 10 servings.

AVGOLEMONO LAMB

Greek egg and lemon sauce is an excellent accompaniment to lamb. The meat should be just slightly pink. Even determined lamb-haters like this preparation.

leg of lamb, 4 to 5 pounds
2 garlic cloves, slivered
2 tablespoons soy sauce
2 tablespoons oil
2¼ cups chicken broth
3 egg yolks

★ ¼ cup reconstituted lemon
  juice
1 teaspoon salt
freshly ground pepper
1 tablespoon cornstarch
2 tablespoons chopped
  parsley

Cut most of the fat and fell from the leg of lamb, or ask your butcher to do it. With a small sharp knife, pierce surface of lamb at 3-inch intervals. Force a sliver of garlic into each slash. Brush with soy sauce, then with oil. Roast in a preheated 425° F. oven for 15 minutes. Reduce heat to 350° F. and roast for 1½ hours. Remove from oven and allow to rest for 15 minutes before carving. Yield: 6 to 8 servings.

Avgolemono Sauce

Bring 2 cups chicken broth to a boil in a small saucepan. Beat egg yolks with lemon juice. Add salt and pepper to taste. Dissolve cornstarch in ¼ cup cold broth and stir into boiling broth. Cook until clear and thickened (see Comment); remove from heat. Beat several tablespoons of this hot sauce into the egg-yolk mixture. When yolks are heated, stir into the rest of sauce. Return to heat and stir over low heat until sauce is heated. Do not boil or eggs will curdle. Stir in parsley. Serve with the lamb. Yield: about 3 cups sauce.

Comment: Cornstarch and arrowroot thicken sauces immediately upon their addition to a hot liquid. If dissolved in a cold liquid, then heated, the sauce takes longer to thicken and requires more cornstarch or arrowroot. The sauce will be at its most glutinous just after clearing. The longer cornstarch and arrowroot cook, the less thick the sauce will be. Flour, on the other hand, requires at least 10 minutes to cook completely if added in the form of a butter and flour paste, molded into little 1-inch balls (*beurre manié*). If flour is cooked in a *roux* before liquid is added, the sauce will only take 2 to 3 minutes of cooking to thicken adequately.

BROILED CARIBBEAN CHICKEN

Broiling chicken is one of the most satisfactory methods of cooking it. The added sauce makes it more elegant.

2 broiler-fryers, 3 pounds each, cut into serving portions
2 tablespoons honey
1 teaspoon dry mustard
1 tablespoon grated fresh gingerroot, or 1 teaspoon ground ginger

★ ⅔ cup pineapple juice
⅓ cup soy sauce
★ ¼ cup reconstituted lemon juice
oil
1 tablespoon cornstarch
2 ounces sherry

Place chicken in a deep bowl. Mix honey, mustard, gingerroot, pineapple juice, soy sauce and lemon juice. Pour over chicken. Marinate for at least 4 hours. Remove from marinade, pat dry, and brush with oil. Broil for 30 minutes, turning often.

Meanwhile, pour marinade into a small saucepan. Heat to boiling. Dissolve cornstarch in sherry; stir into boiling marinade. Cook until clear and thickened into a sauce. Brush on chicken 10 minutes before removing from broiler. Pour sauce over chicken at time of service. Yield: 6 servings.

CARBONNADE OF BEEF

In this Flemish dish, beer replaces wine in the braising process. The addition of brown sugar and vinegar neutralizes the beer. The men in my life have always preferred it to any other braised dish.

★ 1 can (12 oz.) beer
rump of beef, 4 to 5 pounds
½ cup oil, approximately
1 Spanish onion, sliced
2 garlic cloves, crushed
salt and pepper

2 cups beef broth, canned or
    instant
1 tablespoon brown sugar
bouquet garni (p. 69)
1 tablespoon vinegar
beurre manié (p. 69)
½ cup chopped fresh parsley

Open the beer and let it stand for 30 minutes to lose the bubbles. Cut beef into ¼-inch slices. Cut each slice into strips 1 inch x 2 inches. Heat 2 tablespoons oil in a Dutch oven. Quickly brown 1 layer of meat. Drain on paper toweling. Repeat until all meat is browned. Set aside.

Add more oil to Dutch oven. Add onion and sauté until limp. Add garlic and sauté for 2 to 3 more minutes. Add meat strips, season to taste, and toss well to combine meat and vegetables. Add broth and flat beer. Sprinkle with brown sugar, and poke the *bouquet garni* into center of meat. Bring to boil on top of stove; cover. Bake in a preheated 350° F. oven for 1½ hours, or until meat is tender. Do not overcook or meat will disintegrate. Remove meat to a serving dish and keep warm. Add vinegar to the juices in the Dutch oven. Beat in as much *beurre manié* as needed to thicken the sauce. Cook on top of the stove for 10 minutes. Spoon over the meat. Sprinkle with parsley and serve. Yield: 8 servings.

CARNE CON CHOCOLATE

Chocolate used for cooking poultry and meat was traditional in Mexico before the Conquest. Spanish conquistadors adopted it.

3 tablespoons oil
4 pounds beef bottom round
   or rump roast
1 large onion, chopped
2 garlic cloves, crushed
1 teaspoon salt
freshly ground pepper

½ teaspoon ground cloves
bouquet garni (see p. 69)
★ 1 cup seasoned cooking wine
2 cups beef broth, instant or
   canned
1 ounce unsweetened
   chocolate, grated

Heat oil in a Dutch oven. Brown meat on all sides. Remove and drain on paper toweling. Add onion and cook until limp. Add garlic and cook for 1 to 2 minutes. Return meat to pan. Sprinkle with salt, pepper and cloves. Place *bouquet garni* in bottom of pan. Pour wine and broth over all. Bring to a boil on top of the stove. Cover tightly. Bake in a preheated 350° F. oven for 2½ to 3 hours, or until meat is fork-tender. Remove meat. Discard *bouquet garni*. Purée liquid in a blender, or force through a strainer or food mill. Pour into a saucepan and degrease as well as possible (see Note, p.166). Heat liquid to boiling and reduce rapidly over high heat until halved in volume. Add chocolate and cook until melted and smooth. Slice meat, trimming off fat. Arrange slices on an attractive serving platter and pour chocolate sauce over. Yield: 8 servings.

APPLE SQUASH

1 ounce (2 tablespoons) butter
   or margarine
2 scallions, sliced
★ 6 ounces unsweetened apple
   juice

2 cups mashed, cooked winter
   squash
1 teaspoon salt
freshly ground pepper

Heat butter in a 2-quart saucepan. Add scallions and sauté for 2 to 3 minutes. Add apple juice and boil rapidly until reduced to half. Add squash, salt and pepper to taste. Heat over low heat, stirring, until thoroughly heated. Yield: 6 servings.

SWEET-AND-SOUR RED SNAPPER

If red snapper is not available in your area, use bluefish, large trout, rockfish or striped bass instead.

3 pounds red snapper, whole-
 dressed
1 onion, sliced
2 ounces (4 tablespoons)
 butter or margarine

salt and pepper
★ 3 tablespoons frozen orange-
 juice concentrate
1 tablespoon soy sauce

Wash fish cavity. Sauté onion in butter or margarine until limp. Place fish in a greased shallow baking dish. Liberally season fish inside cavity and on surface. Spread onion slices over fish. Drizzle remaining butter from pan evenly across surface. Mix orange-juice concentrate and soy sauce. Drizzle over fish. Bake in a preheated 400° F. oven for 30 minutes. Baste frequently with pan juices. Yield: 4 servings.

PINEAPPLE ZUCCHINI

1½ ounces (3 tablespoons)
 butter or margarine
1 onion, sliced
1 garlic clove, crushed

2 medium-size zucchini, sliced
★ 6 ounces unsweetened
 pineapple juice
salt and pepper

Heat butter in a skillet. Add onion and sauté until limp. Add garlic and sauté for 2 minutes. Add zucchini and cook, uncovered, for 2 minutes. Add pineapple juice, increase heat and continue to cook, tossing constantly, until juice all but evaporates. Season to taste and serve at once. Yield: 4 servings.

BAKED GOODS AND ONE DRINK

CHOCOLATE PEARS

When making this dessert, be sure to drain the pears very well. If too much liquid remains in the fruit, the chocolate coating will gradually slip off if pears are left standing for any length of time. Be sure to start this dish well enough ahead of time so the pears can dry out.

6 whole ripe pears
★ 12 ounces ginger ale
1 cinnamon stick
juice of ½ lemon
12 ounces semisweet
  chocolate bits
¼ cup cream

½ cup ground blanched
  almonds
1 egg white
½ cup raisins, chopped
1 teaspoon ground cinnamon
1 cup chopped pecans

Peel pears, leaving stem ends attached. From root end, carefully remove the core, using a potato peeler. Place pears, root ends down, in an accommodating pot. Add ginger ale, cinnamon stick and lemon juice. Cover and poach for 20 minutes, or until pears are fork tender. Carefully remove them from poaching liquid and drain on paper toweling. Leave pears exposed to the air for at least 4 to 6 hours to dry out.

Place chocolate and cream in the top part of a double boiler. Cook over boiling water until chocolate melts. Mix almonds, egg white, raisins and ground cinnamon. Divide into 6 portions and pack 1 portion into the core cavity of each pear. Using 2 forks, dip each pear into liquid chocolate until evenly coated. Pick chocolate pears up by attached stem and dip lower fourth into chopped pecans. Chill, then serve. Yield: 6 servings.

BOSTON BROWN BREAD

This is an old New England favorite. When I lived in Vermont I used to give these little loaves as Christmas gifts.

1½ cups raisins
1 cup boiling water
★ ½ cup unsweetened prune
   juice
1 ounce (2 tablespoons)
   melted margarine
1 teaspoon vanilla extract
1 egg, lightly beaten

2 cups all-purpose flour
½ teaspoon salt
2 teaspoons baking soda
¾ cup wheat germ
1 cup sugar
½ cup shelled pecans,
   chopped

Drop raisins into 1 cup boiling water and boil for 1½ minutes. Cool. Add prune juice, margarine, vanilla and egg. Sift flour, salt, baking soda, wheat germ and sugar together. Add to egg mixture. Stir in pecans. Heavily grease 4 empty well-washed 1-pound cans with tops cut off, bottoms left on. Spoon enough batter in each can to make it two-thirds full. Place upright in a preheated 350° F. oven and bake for 40 minutes. To remove, slip a knife down sides of cans. If breads do not fall out, cut off bottoms of cans with a can opener and push breads through. Yield: 4 small loaves.

PISTACHIO CAKE

This is an expensive cake but very elegant. The combination of orange concentrate and all the eggs gives it a special quality.

9 eggs, separated, at room
   temperature
dash of salt
1 teaspoon cream of tartar
1⅛ cups of granulated sugar
★ 6 tablespoons frozen orange-
   juice concentrate

grated rind of 2 oranges
1⅛ cups sifted cake flour (see
   p. 158)
2 cups heavy cream
¼ cup confectioners' sugar
½ cup chopped unsalted
   pistachio nuts

Beat egg whites with salt and cream of tartar until soft peaks form (see Note 1, p. 107). Gradually beat in ⅔ cup granulated sugar, and continue to beat until stiff but not dry. Beat egg yolks until very thick and pale. Beat in remaining granulated sugar gradually. Add 4 tablespoons orange-juice concentrate and grated rind of 1 orange. Stir 1 large tablespoon of meringue into the yolks. Pour yolk mixture over top of whites and carefully fold in. Fold in cake flour. Pour into an ungreased 10-inch angel-food pan. Bake in a preheated 300° F. oven for 1 hour. Cool on a rack.

Beat the heavy cream with remaining orange-juice concentrate and orange rind until thick. Add confectioners' sugar and beat until stiff. Spread cake completely with the cream. Sprinkle top with pistachios. Yield: 12 servings.

EGGNOG POUND CAKE

This is a good cake to make when you have leftover eggnog at Christmastime. It matters not a whit that the eggnog is laced with whiskey, rum or brandy—the cake only tastes better.

2 ounces (4 tablespoons) margarine	2 eggs
½ cup blanched almonds, grated	★ 1½ cups commercial eggnog
1 package (18½ oz.) yellow cake mix	2 ounces (¼ cup) melted butter or margarine
⅛ teaspoon grated nutmeg	1 ounce rum (omit if eggnog has been laced)
	confectioners' sugar

Generously grease a 10-inch tube pan with the margarine. Press almonds against the buttered sides and bottom. Combine cake mix, nutmeg, eggs, eggnog, melted butter or margarine and rum. Pour into prepared pan and bake in a preheated 350° F. oven for 45 to 55 minutes, or until a straw stuck in the middle comes out clean. Cool in the pan for 10 minutes. Invert on a cake rack. Serve with a dusting of confectioners' sugar. Yield: 10 to 12 servings.

SANGRÍA

This most refreshing summer drink is wonderful for entertaining.

1 cup strawberries, hulled
2 peaches, peeled and sliced
1 orange, peeled and sliced
1 lemon, sliced

¼ cup sugar
4 ounces brandy
1 bottle of red wine
★ 16 ounces soda water

Place all fruits in a large pitcher. Sprinkle with sugar. Allow to steep for several hours. Pour on all remaining ingredients. Serve icy-cold in large goblets with some of each fruit in each glass. Yield: 3 quarts approximately.

16

COUPONS THAT CAN BE USED FOR LOW-CALORIE RECIPES

There are many ways to convert the recipes in this book to meet the needs of those who are on restricted caloric intake. A little general knowledge about the nutritional content of foods and a large dose of common sense will go a long way.

Here are a number of hints to help the dieter overcome difficulties in planning healthful, low-calorie menus.

1. Onions, mushrooms, garlic, scallions, etc., can be sautéed in far less oil or fat than called for if a lid is placed over the vegetable during the cooking process. The vegetable will steam somewhat, but the taste remains. Constant stirring and tossing will also prevent scorching, as long as the heat is moderately low.

2. Bread-crumb toppings are garnishes adding calories, but basically imparting little flavor to a casserole. A liberal sprinkling of paprika or chopped parsley is a good substitute.

3. When a recipe requires browning meat or poultry in oil before baking in a sauce or dressing, broil for 5 minutes on each side instead. The browning process seals in the meat's natural juices; broiling serves the same purpose.

4. Yogurt, low-calorie cottage cheese and diet sour cream can replace mayonnaise, creamed cottage cheese and commercial sour cream in dressings, sauces and toppings.

5. Artificial bacon bits made from soybeans can substitute for regular bacon if necessary.

6. Butter, margarine and oil can easily be halved in most recipes

without impairing flavor. However, do not do so in baking recipes such as cakes and breads.

7. Commercial whipped toppings made from low-calorie ingredients can be substituted for heavy cream toppings.

As someone who loves food but must watch for problems, I have found that the surest way to control weight is by counting calories. With your doctor's help, decide on the number of calories you require daily to lose approximately 2 pounds a week over a given period. Count every calorie that goes into your mouth. Write them down. Somehow this effort helps you maintain your resolve. Do not deprive yourself of all goodies. If you do, you will never persevere. If you love wine, allow yourself a 4 ounce portion with or before dinner and include those calories in your daily count. Eat desserts occasionally, but let moderation be your guide.

This last chapter is directed to those who want to pare down their figures as well as their food bills.

In the first part you will find recipes from previous chapters that can be adapted to a diet with restricted caloric intake. The coupons issued in this category will be self-evident. The second part offers low-calorie recipes, using coupons regularly issued in many publications.

All calorie counts were taken from the "Handbook of the Nutritional Contents of Foods," prepared for the United States Department of Agriculture, 1975 publication.

ADAPTATIONS OF RECIPES IN PREVIOUS CHAPTERS

APPETIZERS ★★★★★★★★★★★★★★★★★★★★★★★

APPLE-WALNUT APPETIZER (p. 144)

Adaptation: Use low-calorie cottage cheese instead of creamed and ¼ cup of chopped nuts. Calories: 46 per tablespoon.

VEGETABLE DIP (p. 78)

Adaptation: Use yogurt to replace mayonnaise. Calories: 28 per tablespoon.

LUNCHEON OR SUPPER DISHES ★★★★★★
CHEESE SOUFFLÉ (p. 8)

Adaptation: Spread 1 ounce (2 tablespoons) butter or margarine on inside of soufflé dish and cuff instead of 2 ounces. Use 1 ounce (2 tablespoons) butter or margarine for sauce base. When cooling the sauce base, instead of dotting with butter, lay a piece of clear plastic wrap directly over sauce, touching all surfaces, to prevent development of a skin on top. Be sure to use nonfat dry milk for sauce. Calories: 278 per serving.

SEAFOOD SOUFFLÉ (p. 10)

Use recipe as written with above adaptation. Calories: 304 per serving.

GREEN VEGETABLE SOUFFLÉ (p. 10)

Use recipe as written with above adaptation. Calories: 282 per serving.

CHICKEN OR TURKEY SOUFFLÉ (p. 10)

Use recipe as written with above adaptation. Calories: 316 per serving.

MUSHROOM SOUFFLÉ (p. 10)

Use recipe as written with above adaptation. Calories: 311 per serving.

VEGETABLE CASSEROLES ★★★★★★★★★★★★
CAULIFLOWER CHIFFON (p. 45)

Use recipe as written. Calories: 169 per serving.

FAR EAST CELERY (p. 44)

Adaptation: Use ¼ cup bread crumbs, 1 tablespoon almonds and no butter in topping. Calories: 117 per serving.

OKRA CREOLE (p. 55)

Adaptation: Reduce butter or margarine to 1 tablespoon. Cover onion and green pepper with a lid during sautéing. Calories: 89 per serving.

FISH DISHES ★★★★★★★★★★★★★★★★★★★★★★

CIOPPINO (p. 62)

Use recipe as written. Calories: 12 portions: 171 per serving; 15 portions: 137 per serving.

APRICOT-BROILED SWORDFISH (p. 165)

Adaptation: Eliminate 1 tablespoon butter. Use water-packed or low-calorie dietetic canned apricots. Drain and reserve liquid to use in place of apricot nectar. Calories: 360 per serving.

SILKY SALMON CUSTARD (p. 11)

Adaptation: Eliminate butter from peas. Use nonfat dry milk (reconstituted) in place of evaporated milk. Calories: 333 per serving.

SCALLOPED OYSTERS (p. 85)

Adaptation: Use 1 cup cracker crumbs only. Use 1 tablespoon butter or margarine. Calories: 249 per serving.

LOBSTER WITH MELON, AU GRATIN (p. 63)

Adaptation: Make Mornay Sauce (p. 15) with low-fat dry milk. Use only 1 tablespoon butter to sauté onion. Cover them while they cook, keeping heat low. Use ½ cup bread crumbs and 2 tablespoons cheese. Eliminate butter from crumb and cheese topping. Calories: 346 per serving.

SWEET-AND-SOUR RED SNAPPER (p. 186)

Adaptation: Use 1 ounce (2 tablespoons) butter rather than 2 (4 tablespoons). Calories: 249 per serving.

POULTRY AND MEAT DISHES ★★★★★★★★
BROILED CARIBBEAN CHICKEN (p. 183)

Use recipe as written. Calories: 455 per serving.

HONEY-GLAZED CHICKEN (p. 122)

Adaptation: Do not brown chicken in hot oil. Heat broiler and broil 5 minutes on each side, then proceed with the recipe. Calories: 484 per serving.

STEAK TERIYAKI (p. 125)

Adaptation: Use ¼ cup oil rather than ½ cup and only 2 tablespoons honey. Do not eat a starch or bread with this meal; have salad and a green vegetable. Calories: 477 per serving.

DESSERTS ★★★★★★★★★★★★★★★★★★★★★★
BLUEBERRY TAPIOCA (p. 23)

Adaptation: Use ¼ cup sugar rather than ⅓ cup. Calories: 190 per serving.

DESSERT FONDUE (p. 110)

Adaptation: Use angel-food cake. There are approximately 34 calories in a 1½ inch cube of cake. Add 22 calories for each dip of sauce. Calories: 56 per cube of cake.

STRAWBERRY SOUFFLÉ (p. 152)

Adaptation: Buy frozen whole strawberries. There are less calories per package than in the frozen sliced berries. Use ¼ cup sugar rather than ½ cup. Do not serve with sauce. Calories: 121 per serving.

LOW-CALORIE RECIPES

MAIN COURSE DISHES ★★★★★★★★★★★★★

BRAISED VEAL

My husband had an ulcer and was told to lose weight while maintaining his specialized diet. When I was told that veal, fish and poultry were his only meat concessions, I developed this recipe, which he truly enjoyed.

2 medium onions, chopped
1 tablespoon oil
2 carrots, chopped
2 celery ribs, chopped
1 garlic clove, crushed
1 teaspoon paprika
★ 1½ cups chicken broth,
    canned or made from cubes
    or granules

½ cup dry white wine
1 bay leaf
1 teaspoon salt
freshly ground pepper
3 pounds rolled veal roast
¼ cup chopped fresh parsley

Sauté onions in oil in a stove-top-to-oven casserole, covered with a lid, until limp. Add carrots, celery, garlic and paprika. Cook, stirring, for 5 minutes. Pour in broth and wine. Add bay leaf, salt and pepper to taste. Place meat in the pan. Bring liquid to a boil on top of stove. Cover. Place in a preheated 350° F. oven and bake for 2½ hours, or until meat is fork-tender. Remove meat and slice. Discard bay leaf.

Pour liquids into a blender and purée, or force through a food mill. Return meat to casserole, pour sauce over and heat thoroughly. Sprinkle with parsley and serve at once. Yield: 8 servings. Calories: 324 per serving.

VEAL AND EGGPLANT TIMBALES

These meat and vegetable concoctions are baked in large custard cups and unmolded just before serving. The taste may remind you of *moussaka,* a Greek dish made with eggplant and ground lamb.

2 eggplants, 1 pound each
1 tablespoon oil
1 large onion
1 ounce (2 tablespoons) butter
  or margarine
2 cloves garlic, chopped
1 teaspoon crumbled dried
  orégano

1 teaspoon paprika
1 tablespoon snipped fresh dill
1 pound boneless veal, ground
★ ½ pound low-fat cottage
  cheese
3 eggs
salt and pepper

Brush whole eggplants with oil. Bake in a preheated 350° F. oven for 45 minutes, or until soft when pricked with a fork. Cool. Carefully peel off skins and reserve skins. Mash insides in a large bowl. Sauté onion in butter or margarine until limp. Add garlic, orégano, paprika and dill. Cook, stirring, for 2 to 3 minutes. Scrape into eggplant. Add veal, cottage cheese, eggs and seasoning to taste.

Divide eggplant skins equally between 8 greased 1-cup custard cups. Fit skins into cups, allowing them to drape over edges if necessary. Do not worry if cups are not completely lined with eggplant skins; they are only for effect. Fill with veal mixture. Fold excess skins over top of meat filling. Bake in a preheated 350° F. oven for 45 minutes. Unmold on a heated platter. Serve with Lemon Sauce (recipe follows). Yield: 8 servings. Calories: 200 per serving.

Lemon Sauce

★ 1¼ cups chicken broth,
    canned, fresh or frozen
3 egg yolks, beaten

salt and pepper
juice of ½ lemon

Bring broth to a boil. Beat egg yolks with seasoning to taste. Gradually beat in boiling broth. Add lemon juice. Return to heat and cook over very low heat, stirring constantly. Do not boil. When thickened, serve with timbales. Yield: 1½ cups. Calories: 9 per tablespoon.

POACHED TURKEY BREAST WITH DUXELLES STUFFING

This is an alternative for Thanksgiving dinner or at Christmas for dedicated dieters.

★ 5 pounds boned turkey breast
  Duxelles Stuffing (recipe
    follows)
1 medium onion, chopped
1 carrot, chopped
1 small potato, size of an egg,
    cut into 4 pieces

★ 1 cup chicken broth, canned,
    fresh or made from cubes
    or granules
½ cup dry white wine
½ teaspoon salt
freshly ground pepper
bouquet garni (p. 69)
parsley sprigs

Cut boned turkey into 4 thick horizontal slices. Place between sheets of plastic wrap and flatten with the broad side of a meat cleaver or the bottom of an iron skillet. Place a large double thickness of cheesecloth on a board. Lay 1 piece of turkey breast on top. Spread with one third of the stuffing. Place another piece of turkey breast on top and repeat until all stuffing and turkey are used, ending with the last slice of turkey. Tie cheesecloth securely around the stuffed, reshaped turkey breast. Place onion, carrot and potato in the bottom of a heavy-bottomed pot. Add broth, wine, salt, pepper to taste and *bouquet garni*. Place a rack over the vegetables, and place turkey on the rack. Bring liquid to a boil. Cover tightly and simmer for 30 minutes. Mash the potato into the liquids (see Note 1). Cover and simmer for another hour. Remove meat from cooking liquids and let it rest for 20 minutes.

Force braising liquids through a food mill, or whirl in a food processor or blender until puréed. If sauce is too thin, reduce by boiling over high heat until of desired thickness. Untie poached turkey breast. Discard cheesecloth. Slice turkey breast vertically and carefully arrange on a heated platter. Garnish with parsley sprigs and serve with the sauce, or present the sauce separately. Serve Rhubarb and Apple Relish (p. 199) in place of cranberry sauce. Yield: 10 servings. Calories: 437 per serving. Yield: 12 servings. Calories: 364 per serving.

Duxelles Stuffing

4 onions, chopped
2 ounces (4 tablespoons)
   butter or margarine
1 garlic clove, crushed
12 ounces mushrooms,
   chopped
½ cup snipped fresh chives

½ cup chopped fresh parsley
1 teaspoon dried basil
¼ teaspoon crumbled dried
   rosemary (see Note 2)
1 teaspoon salt
freshly ground pepper

Cook onions in butter until limp. Add garlic and mushrooms and sauté for 5 minutes. Add chives, parsley, basil, rosemary, salt and pepper to taste. Cook, stirring, for 5 minutes. Yield: 3 cups.

Note 1: Mashing a small potato into braising stock during the cooking process helps to thicken liquids slightly without adding an additional starch. The calorie count for a potato the size of an egg is about 65. Divided among 10 servings, this adds only 6½ calories per serving.

Note 2: Rosemary is a strong herb; too much will overpower the dish. Add with discretion or, if in doubt, eliminate. It adds a distinct and interesting flavor to the stuffing.

RHUBARB AND APPLE RELISH

Serve with turkey or chicken as a substitute for cranberry sauce. It can also be used in desserts (see p. 206).

½ pound fresh or frozen
   rhubarb
★ ½ cup orange juice
2 firm apples, peeled and
   chopped

1 tablespoon lemon juice
3 envelopes low-calorie
   sweetener

If using fresh rhubarb, cut ribs into ½-inch pieces. Place rhubarb in a saucepan with orange juice and apples. Cook for 10 minutes, or until rhubarb is soft. Add lemon juice and sweetener. Cool completely before serving. Yield: 2½ cups. Calories: 12 per tablespoon.

BAKED LOW-CALORIE CHICKEN

1 broiler-fryer chicken, 3
  pounds
garlic powder
onion powder
★ soy sauce
paprika

★ 1 can (7 oz.) low-calorie
  crushed pineapple
★ ½ cup sliced water chestnuts
2 teaspoons wine vinegar
★ ¼ cup orange juice

Cut chicken into serving portions and place them in a single layer in a baking dish. Sprinkle liberally with garlic powder, onion powder, soy sauce and paprika. Bake uncovered in a preheated 350° F. oven for 20 minutes. Mix all remaining ingredients together. Pour half over chicken and bake for another 20 minutes. Heat remaining mixture and serve as a sauce with chicken. Yield: 4 servings. Calories: 332 per serving.

CHICKEN STIR-FRY

Prepare this in a wok or an electric skillet.

2 pounds chicken breasts,
  boned
2 tablespoons oil
1 medium onion, sliced
¼ pound mushrooms, sliced
1 garlic clove, crushed

★ 1 package (6 oz.) frozen edible
  pea pods (snow peas)
★ 1 cup canned bean sprouts,
  rinsed
★ 2 tablespoons soy sauce
salt and pepper

Remove skin from chicken and cut meat into 1-inch cubes. Heat oil in a skillet or wok. Add onion and sauté, tossing, for 4 minutes. Add mushrooms and garlic and sauté for 3 minutes. Add chicken cubes and cook, tossing, for 10 minutes. Add pea pods and bean sprouts and cook for 5 minutes, or until heated through. Add soy sauce and salt and pepper to taste. Serve at once. Yield: 4 servings. Calories: 311 per serving.

SCALLOP SAUTÉ

1 onion, chopped
1 ounce (2 tablespoons) butter
  or margarine
1 garlic clove

★ 1 package (10 oz.) frozen peas
2 pounds scallops
salt and pepper

Sauté onion in butter until limp. Add garlic and peas and cook for 5 minutes. Add scallops and cook over fairly high heat until scallops become firm and turn white, only a few minutes. Toss constantly so that scallops cook evenly. Do not overcook. Add salt and pepper to taste. Serve at once. Yield: 4 servings. Calories: 295 per servings.

Variation: Scallops are expensive. For a less costly dish, use 2 pounds boneless frozen ocean perch. Defrost it and cut into 1-inch cubes.

TUNA ROLLMOPS

★ 1 can (7 oz.) water-packed
  tuna
½ cup plain yogurt
2 tablespoons chopped
  parsley
½ teaspoon garlic powder
1 teaspoon salt

freshly ground pepper
★ 2 pounds frozen fish fillets,
  defrosted
2 onions, minced
2 carrots, minced
★ 1 cup bottled clam juice
paprika

Drain tuna fish well. Mix with yogurt, parsley, garlic powder, salt and pepper to taste. Divide evenly among fish fillets. Place the portion in the middle of each fillet. Roll fish around stuffing and skewer with a toothpick. Place onions, carrots and clam juice in a casserole. Place tuna rollmops on top. Sprinkle with paprika. Cover casserole tightly and bake in a preheated 400° F. oven for 20 minutes, or until fish flakes when tested with a fork. Pour vegetables and clam juice into a saucepan. Boil rapidly, uncovered, until liquid is reduced by half. Force through a sieve or purée in a blender. Remove toothpicks from rollmops. Pour sauce over fish and serve. Yield: 4 servings. Calories: 340 per serving.

BROILED FISH STEAKS WITH CRESS SAUCE

Fish calorie counts vary from 85 to 268 calories per half pound; it depends on the type of fish chosen. Swordfish is high in calories since it is somewhat oily, and cod is low, with lean flesh. I used kingfish, of the mackerel family, at 238 calories per half pound.

2 pounds fish steaks, ½ inch
   thick (halibut, kingfish,
   salmon, etc.)
1 teaspoon oil
salt and pepper
3 shallots or 1 small onion,
   chopped
1 ounce (2 tablespoons) butter
   or margarine

1 garlic clove, crushed
1 cup finely chopped
   watercress
¼ teaspoon sugar
½ cup dry white wine
★ ½ cup bottled clam juice
   juice of ½ lemon

Wipe steaks with a damp cloth. Place them on an oiled broiling tray, brush with oil, and season to taste. Set aside. Sauté shallots or onion in butter until limp but not browned. Add garlic and watercress. Sprinkle with 1 teaspoon salt, pepper to taste and sugar. Cook for 5 minutes, stirring. Add wine and clam juice. Boil rapidly, uncovered, for 3 to 4 minutes. Add lemon juice. Purée sauce in a blender if you prefer. Broil fish for 5 minutes. Turn and broil on other side for another 5 minutes. Do not overcook. Heat sauce and serve with steaks. Yield: 4 servings. Calories: 336 per serving.

Comment: This aromatic herb, wine and lemon juice sauce resembles the sauces of the *nouvelle cuisine* school, a style of cooking used today in France to replace *haute cuisine,* which is considered too rich, too expensive and too much. Many *nouvelle cuisine* recipes are not exactly low-calorie, since they use cream and butter to enrich sauces in many cases. This recipe goes one step further, eliminating almost all fattening ingredients and still producing a good sauce to complement broiled or poached fish.

DESSERTS ★★★★★★★★★★★★★★★★★★★★★★★★

PEACH PUFF

★ 1 can (1 lb.) water-packed
   pitted peaches
1 tablespoon lemon juice
1 tablespoon lime juice
¼ cup sugar
dash of salt

4 egg yolks
1 envelope unflavored gelatin
4 egg whites
1 cup nondairy whipped
   topping

Drain peaches, reserving ¼ cup of the liquid. Purée peaches in a blender or food processor, or force through a food mill. Mix puréed peaches with lemon juice, lime juice, sugar, salt and egg yolks. Cook over hot water, stirring, until thick. Soften gelatin in reserved ¼ cup peach liquid. Stir into hot custard until gelatin is dissolved. Cool. Beat egg whites until stiff. Fold beaten egg whites and nondairy topping into gelatin. Chill until firm. Yield: 8 servings. Calories: 114 per serving.

LEMON-SHERRY PUDDING

2 tablespoons flour
2 tablespoons sugar
½ teaspoon ground cinnamon
2 whole eggs
2 eggs, separated
★ 1 level teaspoon powdered
   artificial sweetener

1½ ounces sherry
juice of 1 lemon
★ 1 cup reconstituted nonfat dry
   milk
nondairy whipped topping

Sift flour, sugar and cinnamon together. Beat whole eggs, egg yolks, sweetener, sherry and lemon juice. Add milk. Beat egg whites until stiff and fold into first mixture; spoon into a 1½-quart soufflé dish. Set the dish in a pan of hot water and bake in a preheated 350° F. oven for 35 minutes. Serve cold with 1 tablespoon nondairy whipped topping. Yield: 8 servings. Calories: 90 per serving.

NESSELRODE PARFAIT

★ 1 package (2⅝ oz.) strawberry-
flavored low-calorie gelatin
★ 1 package (2⅝ oz.) lime-
flavored low-calorie gelatin
★ 6 teaspoons powdered
artificial sweetener
1 can (1 lb.) water-packed
pitted peaches

1 can (1 lb.) water-packed
pitted cherries
★ 1½ cups nonfat dry milk solids
1 teaspoon vanilla extract
1 teaspoon rum extract
½ cup diced green maraschino
cherries

Prepare gelatin desserts according to package instructions in separate bowls. Add 3 teaspoons powdered sweetener to each bowl.
Chill until syrupy. Drain both fruits, reserving liquids. Dice fruits
finely. Chill reserved juices until icy cold. Pour 1½ cups juices into a
small bowl. Add nonfat dry milk solids, vanilla and rum extracts, and
whip until stiff. Beat syrupy gelatins until fluffy. Add half of the
peaches, half of the cherries and half of the whipped mixture to
each, folding in carefully. Mound alternate layers of the gelatins in
sherbet glasses until filled. Chill. Garnish each glass with 2 teaspoons of green maraschino cherries, and serve. Yield: 12 servings.
Calories: 91.7 per serving.

STRAWBERRY WHIP

1½ envelopes unflavored
gelatin
½ cup water
★ ¾ cup low-calorie ginger ale
1 cup crushed fresh
strawberries

★ 6 envelopes artificial sweetener
2 teaspoons lemon juice
grated rind of 1 lemon
½ cup ice water
★ ½ cup nonfat dry milk solids
6 whole fresh strawberries

Soften gelatin in ½ cup water. Dissolve over hot water. Combine
with ginger ale, crushed strawberries, sweetener, lemon juice and

grated rind. Chill until syrupy. Place ice water in small bowl of an electric mixer. Sprinkle with nonfat dry milk solids. Beat until stiff. Beat partially thickened gelatin mixture until fluffy. Fold in milk topping. Chill. Garnish each serving with a whole strawberry. Yield: 6 servings. Calories: 77 per serving.

RASPBERRY MOUSSE

★ 1 cup low-calorie raspberry preserves
★ 1 package (12 oz.) frozen raspberries, thawed
6 egg whites

1 teaspoon cream of tartar
juice of ½ lemon
1 teaspoon vanilla extract
★ 2 cups low-calorie whipped topping

Strain the preserves to remove seeds. Drain the thawed raspberries but reserve the syrup. Beat egg whites until soft peaks form. Beat in cream of tartar and lemon juice. Whip until stiff. Fold in strained preserves and vanilla. Fold in drained raspberries. Fold in whipped topping. Chill thoroughly. Serve with a spoonful of the reserved raspberry syrup poured over each portion. Yield: 12 servings. Calories: 76½ per serving.

BAKED HONEY CUSTARD

4 eggs
4 tablespoons honey
dash of salt

★ 2 cups reconstituted nonfat dry milk

Beat eggs with honey and salt. Add milk and beat well to mix. Pour into a 1½ quart baking dish. Set dish in a basin of hot water. Bake in a preheated 325° F. oven for 35 minutes, or until a knife inserted in the middle comes out clean. Yield: 8 servings. Calories: 89 per serving.

MERINGUES

3 egg whites, at room
   temperature
dash of salt

1 cup sugar
★ Rhubarb and Apple Relish
   (p. 199)

Beat half of the egg whites until frothy. Add a dash of salt and very gradually add ½ cup sugar. Beat until very stiff. Place a large sheet of brown paper on a cookie sheet. With a pencil and a glass 2½ inches in diameter draw 16 circles, 1 inch apart. Cover each circle with a layer of meringue. Bake in a preheated 250° F. oven for 45 minutes. Beat the remaining egg whites with a dash of salt and ½ cup sugar until very stiff. Remove meringue bases from the oven. Spoon the beaten egg white into a pastry bag fitted with a plain round opening. Pipe an edge of beaten egg white around each baked meringue to a height of 2 inches. If you have no pastry bag, pile up the beaten egg white edges with a teaspoon. Return to the 250° F. oven and bake for another 45 minutes. Cool. Fill with ½ cup of rhubarb and apple relish if so desired. Yield: 16 meringues. Calories: 97 per filled meringue.

Note: These crisp, dry meringues freeze very well.

OEUFS À LA NEIGE

This is a variation of a classic French dessert. Traditionally the eggs (airy little meringues) are served with custard, but apricot sauce reduces the calorie count.

4 egg whites, at room
   temperature
pinch of salt
½ cup sugar

1 teaspoon vanilla extract
★ 4 cups milk, made from nonfat
   dry milk, or liquid skim milk
   Apricot Sauce (recipe follows)

Beat egg whites until foamy. Add salt and the sugar, 1 tablespoon at a time, until all is incorporated. Beat in vanilla. Beat until stiff and glossy. Heat milk in a large skillet to a simmer. Using 2 large spoons, form little meringue pillows by wetting the spoons, scooping up a mound of meringue and rounding off the top with the other wet spoon. Push gently off the first spoon into the milk. Poach for 3 minutes, turn meringues over and poach for another 3 minutes. Do not let the milk boil. Drain meringues on paper toweling. Chill them. Place 2 meringues in each of 8 sherbet glasses. Pour apricot sauce over and serve. Yield: 8 servings. Calories: 27 per meringue; 72 per serving with 1 tablespoon sauce.

Apricot Sauce

2 cups apricot nectar
1 tablespoon lemon juice
½ cup apricot preserves

Place all ingredients in a small saucepan. Heat, stirring, until preserves melt. Cool completely before serving. Yield: 2½ cups. Calories: 18 per tablespoon.

MERINGUE-TOPPED PEARS

★ 1 can (1 lb.) dietetic water-
   packed pear halves
¼ cup brown sugar
1 teaspoon grated lemon rind
4 teaspoons chopped candied
   gingerroot

2 egg whites
⅛ teaspoon cream of tartar
dash of salt
¼ cup granulated sugar
1 teaspoon vanilla extract

Drain pears very well. Place them cavity side up in a baking dish 7 x 11 inches. Mix brown sugar, lemon rind and gingerroot together. Fill each cavity with some of this mixture. Beat egg whites with cream of tartar and salt until soft peaks form. Beat in granulated sugar and vanilla until stiff. Divide meringue evenly among pear halves. Bake pears in a preheated 400° F. oven until meringue browns, 8 to 10 minutes. Yield: 6 servings. Calories: 101 per serving.

Note: Three large fresh pears, peeled, halved and cored, may be used in place of dietetic pear halves. Lay them cut side down in a shallow saucepan and cover with dietetic ginger ale. Cover and simmer for 20 minutes, or until fork tender. Drain pears well and pat dry on paper toweling. Proceed with recipe.

LOW-CALORIE CHEESECAKE

The larger the slices, the higher the calorie count. Divide this cake into 12 portions and you have 169 calories per serving, and with 16 portions, 127 calories each. I would serve 16 portions and help my guests with their calories.

★ ½ cup graham-cracker crumbs
1 teaspoon butter or
   margarine, melted
1 teaspoon brown sugar
1 teaspoon grated orange rind
★ 2 envelopes unflavored gelatin
¾ cup sugar
3 eggs, separated
★ 1½ cups reconstituted nonfat
   dry milk

★ 3 cups ricotta cheese
1 tablespoon orange juice
1 tablespoon lemon juice
1 teaspoon grated orange rind
1 teaspoon grated lemon rind
1 teaspoon vanilla extract
★ 6 ounces frozen sliced
   strawberries (optional)

Mix crumbs, butter or margarine, brown sugar and orange rind. Press evenly over the bottom of an 8-inch springform pan. Bake in a preheated 350° F. oven for 5 minutes. Cool.

Combine gelatin and ¼ cup sugar in the top part of a double boiler. Beat in egg yolks and milk. Cook over boiling water, stirring, until custard coats the spoon and gelatin is dissolved. Remove from heat and chill until syrupy.

Beat ricotta until thick and smooth. Stir in juices, rinds and vanilla. Beat egg whites with remaining ½ cup sugar until stiff but not dry. Stir gelatin custard into cheese mixture. Fold in egg whites. Turn into prepared pan. Chill for at least 8 hours before serving. Garnish with strawberries if desired. Yield: 12 to 16 servings. Calories: 169 per serving for 12 portions; 127 per serving for 16 portions.

INDEX